Doing Business in
Emerging Markets

Doing Business in Emerging Markets

Roadmap for Success

Marcus Goncalves, José Alves,
and Rajabahadur V. Arcot

First published in 2015 by
Business Expert Press, LLC
222 East 46th Street, New York, NY 10017
www.businessexpertpress.com

ISBN-13: 978-1-63157-017-9 (paperback)
ISBN-13: 978-1-63157-018-6 (e-book)

Business Expert Press Economics Collection

Collection ISSN: 2163-761X (print)
Collection ISSN: 2163-7628 (electronic)

Cover and interior design by Exeter Premedia Services Private Ltd.,
Chennai, India

First edition: 2015

10 9 8 7 6 5 4 3 2 1

Printed in the United States of America.

To my forever-beautiful wife, Carla, and my son Samir,
both living here on earth, and to my children
Andrea and Joshua, who are now living in Heaven.

To God be the glory!

Marcus Goncalves
Summer 2014

I would like to dedicate to my loving parents
Venkataraman V. Arcot and Tarabai V. Arcot,
now living in Heaven.

Rajabahadur V. Arcot

Abstract

Doing Business in Emerging Markets reflects the challenges and opportunities facing international businesses and professionals when operating in emerging markets, particularly in the wake of the financial crisis of 2008. This book is filled with valuable information and real-world facts and examples from across the globe. It covers all the key topics on conducting business in emerging markets, addressing important aspects of entering a new market, as well as post-entry issues and strategies, such as dealing with corruption, the application of the United States Foreign Corrupt Practice Act (FCPA), international market research and more, demonstrating how the emerging market context challenges traditional international business theories and even best practices.

Marcus Goncalves, Fall 2014.

Keywords

emerging markets, FCPA, global corruption, global crime, international business, international marketing research

Contents

Acknowledgments

There were many people who helped us during the process of writing this book. It would be impossible to keep track of them all. Therefore, to all that we have forgotten to list, please don't hold it against us!

We would like to thank Dr. Patrick Barron, professor at the Graduate School of Banking at the University of Wisconsin, Madison, and of Austrian economics at the University of Iowa, in Iowa City for his contributions on the issue of currency wars in chapter 5. Many thanks also to ambassador M.K. Bhadrakumar, former diplomat in the Indian Foreign Service with assignments in the Soviet Union, South Korea, Sri Lanka, Germany, Afghanistan, Pakistan, Uzbekistan, Kuwait, and Turkey for his valuable insights and contributions to foreign policy issues in the MENA region.

CHAPTER 1

Entering an Emerging Market

Overview

Entering an emerging market is not easy. In our experience in teaching this topic, consulting for several multinational corporations around the world, and being a practitioner ourselves, we find that emerging markets are tough to enter. Government interference, backward infrastructure, and a lack of skilled workers require a lot of patience, perseverance, and specialized assistance. Opportunities in the emerging markets come with their own set of challenges. For instance, often lack of education of the workforce translates into thwarted growth being curbed by a lack of a skilled workforce. Other challenges that arise are legal frameworks with regard to trade policies, which may be absent or underdeveloped, or tendencies for political paternalism or blatant interferences, which we see in India and Latin America.

Compare the above to the advanced economies, which, despite the fact that growth has been flat to negative since 2008, continues to supersede emerging markets. When looking at the EU, the 27-member countries allow for labor mobility and a free flow of goods without tariff or nontariff restrictions. Furthermore, the workers in many EU countries are highly educated and have conferred great reputations for their economies. "German engineering" is well known around the world for its high level of quality, the same cannot be said for Indian or Russian engineering.

India has been making progress in opening its economy, but its political response to a much-needed foreign investment is troubling. Large foreign retailers such as IKEA are willing to employ thousands of Indians, but politicians continue to fret about mom-and-pop stores and other small businesses that may be displaced. In 2012, politicians forbade IKEA from selling half its product line in India. In 2012, the deputy chief minister for Punjab went as far as to declare that there was no need for foreign-owned discount retail chains because there are already a multitude of stores selling cheap goods.[1]

Foreign investors become confused and frustrated with these types of patriarchal decisions such as these. Although many nations have transitioned from autocratic rule to democracies with free markets, some continue to dabble in market interference. Take Argentina as an example, where President Cristina Fernández de Kirchner, to prevent a run on the peso by Argentines, has put strict currency controls in place. It is not wonder that in an annual World Bank study titled *Doing Business* (2013), New Zealand, Singapore, and Hong Kong ranked first, second, and third place respectively in protecting investors, while Argentina ranks 98.[2]

Emerging markets such as India and China have huge and growing populations and thus demand rapid growth rate if they are to make any headway in social development. If India's economic growth falls below six percent the nation would be in crisis, whereas in most advanced economies, such as the United States, if the economy grew at that rate it would risk overheating.

India can barely keep up with educating its rising populations. It needs as many as 1,000 new universities and 35,000 new colleges if it is to achieve its stated goal of raising post-secondary enrollment from 12 percent today to 30 percent by 2020. Meanwhile, Mexico is turning out more engineers and engineering technicians a year than Germany, and it must scramble to ensure they all get jobs. To fail would be to spawn social unrest.

Another key factor when considering entering emerging markets is the distance between emerging markets, which can hamper trade. One study found that a 10 percent increase in distance between north-to-north traders reduces trade by 10 percent; the same distance between south-to-south traders reduces trade by 17 percent.[3]

An improved policy would make an important difference in resolving such problems but emerging market have yet to demonstrate serious desires for true bilateral cooperation. Although the ASEAN nations have a trade agreement, it has yet to yield much economic improvement, as the bloc has yet to turn their loose organization into a trading block, even though economic integration has been touted as a central pillar.

Public administration in emerging markets has much to be desired. The 2013 *Doing Business*[4] study by the World Bank ranks Brazil, Russia, India, China, and South Africa (BRICS) as 116th, 92nd, 134th, 96th, and 41th respectively out of 189 countries.

Infrastructure remains a significant problem in most emerging markets. China continues to invest heavily in roads, railways, and ports, but elsewhere the progress is weak. India has called for $1 trillion in infrastructure modernization but it lacks the funds to do so independently and its politicians remain suspicious of external sources of capital. The situation is no different in Latin America, in fact, it is arguably worse, as 80 percent of Latin Americans live in cities, compared to fewer than half of Asians. The need for modern urban infrastructure is urgent. Brazil, for instance, wants to improve its infrastructure, which is a bottleneck for the outflow of many of its export products, but it is moving glacially. It has been so slow that Sao Paulo's underground rapid transit system covers only one-tenth of the distance of the one in Seoul, South Korea.*

Does all this mean that foreign investors should avoid trading with or investing in emerging markets? On the contrary, however, any organized program of opening up to emerging markets must include specialized expertise, on-the-ground knowledge, local partnerships, and, most of all, patience.

Why Multinationals Fail in Emerging Markets

Pacek and Thorniley[5] identified an exhaustive range of factors contributing to the failure of companies from advanced economies into emerging markets. These factors may be divided into external and internal factors and almost all are related to strategic and leadership issues:

- Leaders fail to consider emerging markets as an integral part of strategy and acknowledge that such markets need to be approached with a distinct set of criteria for judging progress and success.

---

* Ibidem.

- Top leaders fail to commit sufficient resources to get businesses established and growing in emerging markets, or acknowledge that it is never a short-term affair.
- Companies fail to appoint a head manager for emerging markets and often assign this responsibility to an international manager who is responsible for markets in both developed and emerging countries. The problem with this is that operational approaches are distinct in each of these markets.
- Companies fail to understand that business is driven by heads of regions and business units rather than by heads of functional areas. While the former have a focus and appreciation for the emerging markets, the latter tend also to be interested in developed markets.
- Companies do not acknowledge that emerging markets operate under distinct business models and structures, and often merely transfer practices tested in developed markets without considering adaptation.
- The board members of many companies have limited diversity in terms of culture and ethnic background and do not develop sufficient appreciation for the peculiarities of emerging markets.
- Multinationals underestimate the potential and often early competition from smaller international and domestic companies, thus never accepting that they may be destined as a follower in emerging markets.
- Economic and political crisis also exist in emerging markets and have a significant impact on business performance. Top managers need to understand this, be prepared to adapt and introduce new tactics rather than changing strategy, which despite having short-term success, tend to be the wrong approach in the long term.
- Companies get alarmed by short-term slippages and cut costs to attain favorable temporary results, yet this is likely to have a structural impact on strategy implementation and long-term results.
- Companies set unrealistic targets to achieve, which leave managers with limited maneuvering space and short-lived careers.

- Companies fail to recognize that entering the market early is fundamental in establishing networks, developing brands and learning the larger context from which it will operate.
- Senior leaders fail to recognize that developing a network of reliable contacts often requires establishing friendships with locals, which requires time and visibility in emerging markets.
- Companies fail to empower regional and country managers and delegate decision-making power to local managers.
- Foreign companies fail to recognize that emerging markets are more price-sensitive and often stick to their pricing structures instead of adapting to local sensitivities.
- International firms fail to recognize that their product portfolio is not tailored to the lower and middle segments of emergent markets and do not develop innovations that are context-oriented.
- Foreign companies underestimate the competition from local companies in emergent markets. Local companies understand better than anyone about local markets, sometimes employ dubious practices, and often have the support of local governments.
- One of the largest obstacles that foreign companies face may be the unwillingness to change long-standing business practices.
- Another challenge is to appoint senior managers who are not familiar with the local market, culture, and language in emerging countries.
- Multinationals that focus too much on the larger emerging markets, such as BRIC, may neglect smaller markets and miss better-suited opportunities.
- The fact that demand is volatile and unpredictable in emergent markets may discourage multinationals, which often expect reliable market information.

The failure factors are numerous and diverse but as Pacek and Thorniley noted it all boils down to a lack of adequate market entry preparation. Preparation requires companies to continuously research the external environment and know how to use internal resources to take advantage of opportunities. Hence, a preliminary audit that focuses on external and internal factors is essential. The external factors may be examined by posing questions concerning the market, the political environment, the economic environment, and the business environment, as depicted in Table 1.1.

Table 1.1 External factors and sample questions

Understanding the market	
Market potential	• How large and wealthy is the market? • Is there unsatisfied demand for the product/service?
Understanding local consumers/customers	• Who are the consumers/customers? What are their characteristics? • How do consumers make their decisions?
Reaching the consumer/customer	• How difficult/easy is it to reach potential consumers/customers? • How do competitors and non-competitors reach their customers?
Competition	• Which competitors are already operating in the market? • How strong are these competitors?
Lessons learned by noncompetitors	• What do noncompetitors say about the business environment in the country? • What have been the largest obstacles to successful operations?
Local culture	• What aspects of local culture are relevant to running a successful local business?
Understanding the political and economic environment	
Economic outlook	• How sustainable is economic growth? • What is driving economic growth?
Political outlook	• What is the level of political risk and how will or might affect the business?
Government policies	• Does the government allow a level playing filed? • Is the government in the hands of local lobbies?
Understanding the business environment	
Finance	• Is it possible to finance operations locally? • What access do customers/consumers have to finance?
Labor market	• What are the wage/salary rates for the employees who will be needed? • What are the most effective ways of recruiting local employees?

Understanding the business environment	
Taxation	• What are the current levels of taxation? • What is the outlook for tax incentives?
Legal environment	• How effective and efficient is the local judiciary? • Is there any hope that the legal system will improve?
Bureaucratic obstacles to business	• What are the most common bureaucratic obstacles for business? • How easy or difficult it is to set up business in the country?
Crime and corruption	• Is crime a problem for business? • What is the level of corruption?
Infrastructure	• What is the quality of local transport infrastructure? • And telecommunications?
Foreign trade environment	• Is the country a WTO member? • Does it belong to any trading blocs or regional free-trade areas?
Cost of building a business and brand	• How expensive is it to build a brand? • How much time will it take to do what is necessary to get the business off the ground?

Table 1.2 Internal factors and sample questions

Resources	• How much time and money will be required? • Is the CEO committed to support business development and provide necessary resources? And the senior managers? • What human resources are needed?
Products	• Is the product portfolio right for the market? • Will investment be available for developing new products?
Organization	• Will existing internal processes and operational practices help or hinder what is planned? • What existing capabilities can be drawn?
Risks	• Can the risks that have been identified be managed? • How would entry be financed?

By the same token, the internal factors must inquire about resources, products, organization, and risks, as depicted in Table 1.2.

Having done a preliminary external and internal audit, managers need to prepare a business proposal describing what to do, how to do it, by when, and resources required. Business must then ask themselves whether there are similar or better opportunities available in other emerging markets. How then, can we compare the potential of different emerging markets?

Ranking Emerging Markets

According to the GlobalEdge[6] team at the International Business Center (IBC) at The Eli Broad Graduate School of Management, Michigan State University, there are three main reasons why emerging markets are attractive. They are target markets, manufacturing bases, and sourcing destinations.

As target markets they present a growing middle class with substantial demand for consumer products and services. They are also excellent targets for electronics, automobiles, and healthcare services. The textile (machinery) industry in India is huge, oil and gas exploration plays a vital role in Russia, agriculture is a major sector in China, and airplanes are almost everywhere.

As manufacturing bases they present advantages such as low-wages, high quality labor for manufacturing and assembly operations. South Africa is a key source for industrial diamonds; Thailand has become an important manufacturing location for Japanese MNEs such as Sony, Sharp, and Mitsubishi; Malaysia and Taiwan are home to manufacturing of semiconductors by MNEs such Motorola, Intel, and Philips; and in Mexico and China we find platforms for consumer electronics and auto assembly.

As sourcing destinations the emerging markets also are using their advantages to attract MNEs. MNEs have established call centers in Eastern Europe, India, and the Philippines; Dell and IBM outsource certain technological functions to knowledge workers in India; and Brazil is a leading raw material supplier namely in oil and agriculture.

The Emerging Market Potential Index (EMPI) was based on Cavusgil[7] indexing approach and developed by the GlobalEdge team to assess the market potential of Emerging Markets. As shown in Table 1.3, EMPI is based on eight dimensions: market size, market growth rate, market intensity, market consumption capacity, commercial infrastructure, economic freedom, market receptivity, and country risk. Each dimension is measured using various indicators and are weighed in determining the overall index. The result is a score on a scale from 1 to 100.

Table 1.3, based on Cavugil, Kiyak, and Yeniyurt[8] indicator, is useful in that it provides the relative position of each country but is lacking

Table 1.3 Market potential index (MPI), 2014

Overall rank	Country	Overall score	Market size	Market intensity	Market growth rate	Market consumption capacity	Commercial infrastructure	Market receptivity	Economic freedom	Country risk
1	China	100	100	4	100	98	56	9	23	80
2	Hong Kong	56	2	100	62	31	96	100	100	95
3	Japan	54	21	77	49	100	81	9	70	90
4	Canada	53	9	80	55	63	89	65	77	90
5	Singapore	50	2	76	76	33	83	89	70	100
6	Germany	48	12	79	48	85	94	18	71	83
7	India	46	37	36	77	57	14	9	47	64
8	Switzerland	41	2	94	52	48	89	36	78	90
9	United Kingdom	41	8	85	43	69	93	15	72	75
10	South Korea	41	10	59	67	60	78	21	63	83
11	France	41	10	72	46	72	94	12	61	75
12	Australia	41	5	75	59	60	96	14	79	83
13	United Arab Emirates	38	2	66	91	37	88	43	43	74
14	Norway	37	3	84	62	49	82	16	68	90

(Continued)

Table 1.3 Market potential index (MPI), 2014 (Continued)

Overall rank	Country	Overall score	Market size	Market intensity	Market growth rate	Market consumption capacity	Commercial infrastructure	Market receptivity	Economic freedom	Country risk
15	Russia	36	19	41	71	51	81	8	28	64
16	Austria	36	2	77	51	51	97	19	70	83
17	Netherlands	36	3	63	40	53	84	40	71	75
18	Belgium	36	3	69	50	44	80	43	67	75
19	Sweden	35	3	67	52	53	90	16	70	90
20	Brazil	34	18	48	62	41	58	6	50	69
21	New Zealand	33	2	67	62	41	88	14	78	83
22	Denmark	33	2	68	39	54	94	18	73	83
23	Ireland	32	1	55	41	42	100	36	73	75
24	Italy	32	8	72	33	65	74	11	59	59
25	Mexico	31	10	61	62	39	40	23	54	70

analysis as it does not provide what the data actually mean, what managers can do with this data.

From Indicators to Institutions

It is common wisdom that size and growth potential are the two best criteria to select an emerging market. Not so for Khanna and Palepu[9] who argue that lack of institutions, such as distribution systems, credit cards systems, or data research firms, is the primary factor to consider when entering into an emerging market. For them, the fact that emerging markets have poor institutions, thus, inefficient business operations, present the best business opportunities for companies operating in such dynamic markets. However, the way businesses enter into emerging markets is different, and are contingent upon variations presented by the institutions and the abilities of the firms.

Khanna and Palepu point out that the use of composite indexes to assess the potential of emerging markets, as executives often do, has limited use because these indicators do not capture the soft infrastructures and institutions. These composite indexes are useful in ranking market potential of countries when and only these countries have similar institutional environments. When soft infrastructures differ we must then look at the institutional context in each market. In fact when comparing the composite indexes of the BRIC countries we find that they are similar in terms of competitiveness, governance, and corruption. Yet the key success factors for companies in the BRIC differ significantly from country to country. Take for example the retail chain industry.

In China and Russia retail chain operators, both multinationals and local companies, converge in urban and semi-urban areas. In contrast, in Brazil very few multinational retail chains are located in urban centers, and in India we find even fewer international retail chains due to government restrictions that until 2005, did not allow foreign direct investment in this industry. Thus, when looking at the economic indicators of the BRIC countries we find that increased consumption provides opportunities for retail operators.

Best Opportunities Fill in Institutional Voids

From an institutional view the market is a transactional place embedded in information and property rights, and emerging markets are a place where one or both of these features are underdeveloped.* Most definitions of emerging markets are descriptive based on poverty and growth indicators. In contrast a structural definition as proposed by Khanna and Palepu points to issues that are problematic therefore allowing an immediate identification of solutions. Moreover, a structural definition allows us not only to understand commonalities among emerging markets but also to understand what differentiates each of these markets. Finally, a structural approach provides a more precise understanding of the market dynamics that genuinely differentiates emerging markets from advanced economies.

To illustrate, let us contrast the equity capital markets of South Korea and Chile. According to the IFC definition, Korea is not an emerging market because it is an OECD member, however, when we look at its equity capital market we notice that until recently it was not functioning well, in other words it has an institutional void. Chile on the other hand is considered an emerging market in Latin America but has an efficient capital market, thus no institutional void appears in this sector. However, Chile has institutional voids in other markets such as the products market.

Strategy formulation in emerging markets must begin with a map of institutional voids. What works in the headquarters of a multinational company does not per se work in new locations with different institutional environments. The most common mistake companies do when entering emerging markets is to overestimate the importance of past experience. This common error reflects a recency bias, or when a person assumes that recent successful experiences may be transferred to other places. A manager incorrectly assumes that the way people are motivated in one country would be the same in the new country (context). It may be assumed that everyone likes to be appreciated, but the way of expressing appreciation depends on the institutional environment. Khanna and Palepu point out that the human element is the cornerstone of operating

---

* Ibidem.

in new contexts. Ultimately, human beings, who provide a mix of history, culture, and interactions, create institutions.

In short, based on Khanna and Palepu's institutional approach to emerging markets it is necessary to answer several questions. Which institutions are working and missing? Which parts of our business model (in the home country) would be affected by these voids? How can we build competitive advantage based on our ability to navigate institutional voids? How can we profit from the structural reality of emerging markets by identifying opportunities to fill voids, serving as market intermediaries?

Strategies for Emerging Markets

The work of Khanna and Palepu indicates that there are four generic strategic choices for companies operating in emerging markets:

- Replicate or adapt?
- Compete alone or collaborate?
- Accept or attempt to change market context?
- Enter, wait, or exit?

Emerging markets attract two competing types of firms, the developed market-based multinationals and the emerging market-based companies. Both bring different advantages to fill institutional voids. Multinational enterprises (MNEs) bring brands, capital talent, and resources, whereas local companies contribute with local contacts and context knowledge. Because they have different strengths and resources, foreign and domestic firms will compete differently and must develop strategies accordingly.

Table 1.4 summarizes the strategies and options for both multinational firms and local companies.

An example of how companies fill institutional voids is provided by Anand P. Arkalgud (2011).[10] Road infrastructure in India is still underdeveloped in terms of quality and connectivity. Traditionally, Tata Motors has been the dominant player in the auto industry but when it started to receive competition from Volvo in the truck segment and by Japanese auto makers in the car segment Tata responded. It created a mini-truck that not only provided more capacity and safety than the two and

Table 1.4 Responding to institutional voids

Strategic choice	Options for multinationals from developed countries	Options for emerging market-based companies
Replicate or adapt?	• Replicate business model, exploiting relative advantage of global brand, credibility, know-how, talent, finance, and other factor inputs. • Adapt business models, products, or organizations to institutional voids.	• Copy business model from developed countries. • Exploit local knowledge, capabilities, and ability to navigate institutional voids to build tailored business models.
Compete alone or collaborate?	• Compete alone. • Acquire capabilities to navigate institutional voids through local partnerships or JVs.	• Compete alone. • Acquire capabilities from developed markets through partnerships or JVs with multinational companies to bypass institutional voids.
Accept or attempt to change market context?	• Take market context as given. • Fill institutional voids in service of own business.	• Take market context as given. • Fill institutional voids in service of own business.
Enter, wait, or exit?	• Enter or stay in market spite of institutional voids. • Emphasize opportunities elsewhere.	• Build business in home market in spite of institutional voids. • Exit home market early in corporate history if capabilities unrewarded at home.

Source: Khanna and Palepu (2010)

three-wheeled pollutant vehicles used to access market areas but also an environmentally sound vehicle, one that could easily maneuver U-turns in such narrow streets.

Another case in India involved Coca Cola, who discovered that their beverages were being sold "warm." Coca Cola realized that it needed a solution to sell its product "chilled." The reason for the warm bottles was that electricity supplies in these remote locations were unstable especially in summer periods. Thus the company developed a solar-powered cooler and partnered with a local refrigeration company.

Tarun Khanna and Krishna Palepu propose the following five contexts as a framework in assessing the institutional environment of any country. The five contexts include the markets needed to acquire input (product, labor, and capital) and markets needed to sell output. This is referred to as the products and services market. In addition to these three dimensions the framework includes a broader sociopolitical context defined by political and social systems and degrees of openness. When applying the framework managers need to ask a set of questions in each dimension. An example of these questions is indicated in Table 1.5 below.

Table 1.5 Framework to assess institutional voids

Institutional dimension	Questions
Product markets	1. Can companies easily obtain reliable data on customer tastes and purchase behaviors? Are there cultural barriers to market research? Do world-class market research firms operate in the country? 2. Can consumers easily obtain unbiased information on the quality of the goods and services they want to buy? Are there independent consumer organizations and publications that provide such information? 3. Can company's access raw materials and components of good quality? Is there a deep network of suppliers? Are there firms that assess suppliers' quality and reliability? Can companies enforce contracts with suppliers? 4. How strong are the logistics and transportation infrastructures? Have global logistics companies set up local operations? 5. Do large retail chains exist in the country? If so, do they cover the entire country or only the major cities? Do they reach all consumers or only wealthy ones? 6. Are there other types of distribution channels, such as direct-to-consumer channels and discount retail channels that deliver products to customers? 7. Is it difficult for multinationals to collect receivables from local retailers? 8. Do consumers use credit cards, or does cash dominate transactions? Can consumers get credit to make purchases? Are data on customer creditworthiness available? 9. What recourse do consumers have against false claims by companies or defective products and services? 10. How do companies deliver after-sales service to consumers? Is it possible to set up a nationwide service network? Are third-party service providers reliable? 11. Are consumers willing to try new products and services? Do they trust goods from local companies? How about from foreign companies? 12. What kind of product-related environmental and safety regulations are in place? How do the authorities enforce those regulations?

(Continued)

Table 1.5 Framework to assess institutional voids (Continued)

Institutional dimension	Questions
Labor markets	1. How strong is the country's education infrastructure, especially for technical and management training? Does it have a good elementary and secondary education system as well?
	2. Do people study and do business in English or in another international language, or do they mainly speak a local language?
	3. Are data available to help sort out the quality of the country's educational institutions?
	4. Can employees move easily from one company to another? Does the local culture support that movement? Do recruitment agencies facilitate executive mobility?
	5. What are the major post recruitment-training needs of the people that multinationals hire locally?
	6. Is pay for performance a standard practice? How much weight do executives give seniority, as opposed to merit, in making promotion decisions?
	7. Would a company be able to enforce employment contracts with senior executives? Could it protect itself against executives who leave the firm and then compete against it? Could it stop employees from stealing trade secrets and intellectual property?
	8. Does the local culture accept foreign managers? Do the laws allow a firm to transfer locally hired people to another country? Do managers want to stay or leave the nation?
	9. How are the rights of workers protected? How strong are the country's trade unions? Do they defend workers' interests or only advance a political agenda?
	10. Can companies use stock options and stock-based compensation schemes to motivate employees?
	11. Do the laws and regulations limit a firm's ability to restructure, downsize, or shut down?
	12. If a company were to adopt its local rivals' or suppliers' business practices, such as the use of child labor, would that tarnish its image overseas?
Capital markets	1. How effective are the country's banks, insurance companies, and mutual funds at collecting savings and channeling them into investments?
	2. Are financial institutions managed well? Is their decision making transparent? Do noneconomic considerations, such as family ties, influence their investment decisions?
	3. Can companies raise large amounts of equity capital in the stock market? Is there a market for corporate debt?
	4. Does a venture capital industry exist? If so, does it allow individuals with good ideas to raise funds?

Institutional dimension	Questions
Capital markets	5. How reliable are sources of information on company performance? Do the accounting standards and disclosure regulations permit investors and creditors to monitor company management? 6. Do independent financial analysts, rating agencies, and the media offer unbiased information on companies? 7. How effective are corporate governance norms and standards at protecting shareholder interests? 8. Are corporate boards independent and empowered, and do they have independent directors? 9. Are regulators effective at monitoring the banking industry and stock markets? 10. How well do the courts deal with fraud? 11. Do the laws permit companies to engage in hostile takeovers? Can shareholders organize themselves to remove entrenched managers through proxy fights? 12. Is there an orderly bankruptcy process that balances the interests of owners, creditors, and other stakeholders?
Political and social system	1. To whom are the country's politicians accountable? Are there strong political groups that oppose the ruling party? Do elections take place regularly? 2. Are the roles of the legislative, executive, and judiciary clearly defined? What is the distribution of power between the central, state, and city governments? 3. Does the government go beyond regulating business to interfering in it or running companies? 4. Do the laws articulate and protect private property rights? 5. What is the quality of the country's bureaucrats? What are bureaucrats' incentives and career trajectories? 6. Is the judiciary independent? Do the courts adjudicate disputes and enforce contracts in a timely and impartial manner? How effective are the quasi-judicial regulatory institutions that set and enforce rules for business activities? 7. Do religious, linguistic, regional, and ethnic groups coexist peacefully, or are there tensions between them? 8. How vibrant and independent is the media? Are newspapers and magazines neutral, or do they represent sectarian interests? 9. Are nongovernmental organizations, civil rights groups, and environmental groups active in the country? 10. Do people tolerate corruption in business and government? 11. What role do family ties play in business? 12. Can strangers be trusted to honor a contract in the country?
Openness	1. Are the country's government, media, and people receptive to foreign investment? Do citizens trust companies and individuals from some parts of the world more than others?

(Continued)

Table 1.5 Framework to assess institutional voids (Continued)

Institutional dimension	Questions
Openness	2. What restrictions does the government place on foreign investment? Are those restrictions in place to facilitate the growth of domestic companies, to protect state monopolies, or because people are suspicious of multinationals?
	3. Can a company make greenfield investments and acquire local companies, or can it only break into the market by entering into joint ventures? Will that company be free to choose partners based purely on economic considerations?
	4. Does the country allow the presence of foreign intermediaries such as market research and advertising firms, retailers, media companies, banks, insurance companies, venture capital firms, auditing firms, management consulting firms, and educational institutions?
	5. How long does it take to start a new venture in the country? How cumbersome are the government's procedures for permitting the launch of a wholly foreign-owned business?
	6. Are there restrictions on portfolio investments by overseas companies or on dividend repatriation by multinationals?
	7. Does the market drive exchange rates, or does the government control them? If it's the latter, does the government try to maintain a stable exchange rate, or does it try to favor domestic products over imports by propping up the local currency?
	8. What would be the impact of tariffs on a company's capital goods and raw materials imports? How would import duties affect that company's ability to manufacture its products locally versus exporting them from home?
	9. Can a company set up its business anywhere in the country? If the government restricts the company's location choices, are its motives political, or is it inspired by a logical regional development strategy?
	10. Has the country signed free-trade agreements with other nations? If so, do those agreements favor investments by companies from some parts of the world over others?
	11. Does the government allow foreign executives to enter and leave the country freely? How difficult is it to get work permits for managers and engineers?
	12. Does the country allow its citizens to travel abroad freely? Can ideas flow into the country unrestricted? Are people permitted to debate and accept those ideas?

Cases[11]

A series of recent case studies of Western companies operating in emerging markets illustrates the diversity and complexity of marketing issues faced in areas such as socio-cultural dynamics, market orientation, brand strategies, product development, market entry, communications, and social media (Mutum, Roy, and Kipnis, 2014). Even though most cases in Mutum et al's (2014) research have lessons that are relevant for this chapter, we specifically draw on a selected few cases directly related to market entry.

Principles:

- Speed up new product development for firms aiming to increase export involvement
- Pressure for business responsiveness demands adaptation capabilities to the local environment
- Diverse range of marketing strategies

Case: Kraft–Cadbury in India

In 2010, the U.S. based Kraft Foods, Inc. acquired Cadbury, a UK-based confectionary maker. Cadbury was founded in 1824 and as of 2009 it held a 10 percent share of the global market for chocolate, gums, and candy industry. It had a strong presence in emerging markets where it held a dominant position in relation to other major competitors. One particular market where Cadbury had a well-established presence for over 60 years is India. One reason why Kraft Foods acquired Cadbury was precisely to access to emerging markets, namely India and China, where Kraft's presence was marginal. Prior to acquiring Cadbury, Kraft did not have any meaningful presence in India, and currently it is entering India's packaged food market with new innovative products and packages. For example the Kraft's Oreos brand has been repackaged using Cadbury's banner and is being funneled through Cadbury's network of mom-and-pop stores.

Case: McDonalds in India

McDonalds entered India in 1996 and by 2011 it had opened 211 restaurants in tier 1 and tier 2 cities across the country. In a country where people are biased toward their own food habit and cultures, one might expect foreign food retailing companies to face challenges upon entering India. However, while this was hitherto the scenario, it has changed recently with the new lifestyles and food consumption patterns in India, namely due to increased disposable income of middle and upper classes. McDonalds took advantage of these opportunities by adapting the menu to Indian tastes and offering home delivery.

Conclusion

Entry mode* is determined by product, market and organizational factors. In regard to products, companies need to know whether the nature and range of the product, along with available marketing strategies will require any adaptation. If so, they should consider a partner in that emerging market. Usually a higher level of control and resource commitment in the foreign market is required for new or wider product offerings as well as higher levels of adaptation. When taking into account market factors managers need to consider physical distance and experience, as well as identify appropriate marketing strategies and distribution channels, and priorities in revenues, costs, and profits.

Organizationally, major concerns are communication with foreign operations and control of overseas activities. One particular concern in foreign markets is the control of assets. Firms will prefer to internalize activities where there is a higher chance of opportunism by the partners in the emerging market.

---

* http://globaledge.msu.edu/reference-desk/online-course-modules/market-research-and-entry

CHAPTER 2

The Importance of Market Research and Business Intelligence

Overview

In recent years, the global economy has undergone transformational changes. Countries, which benefited from industrialization and emerged as advanced economies, are experiencing a slowdown and their financial markets are under considerable stress. On the other hand, after many *lost decades*, a few other countries, now pegged as emerging economies, have started making remarkable progress on the GDP growth front. While some emerging countries in Asia, such as Korea and Taiwan, have made economic progress by latching onto the growth wave unleashed by the electronic, information, communication technology industry, others have made progress by expanding their trade* with developed countries.

In the midst of these changes, the global economy also have experienced some major crises and resets, such as the Asian Financial Crisis, the U.S. housing bubble, followed by the global financial crisis, and the European sovereign debt crisis, with some of the above happening in quick succession. Due to these economic and financial crises, the real economy and financial markets suffered, people lost jobs, and growth slackened. As discussed in earlier chapters, while most advanced economies continue to struggle to recover from these developments, emerging economies have emerged more resilient;[1] either they recovered more quickly[2] or managed to avoid being hurt as much. Following the global financial crisis,

---

* http://en.wikipedia.org/wiki/Trade_and_development (last accessed on December 3, 2013).

some analysts even thought that the emerging economies could decouple and chart their own growth paths. However, later developments, such as the worsening of current account deficits for some emerging countries, such as India, a strengthening of the BRIC countries' currencies resulting from U.S. qualitative easing (QE) programs, and their subsequent drastic weakening from the expected gradual withdrawal of QE have clearly established that we are truly living in a flat and interconnected world. We believe these developments have reinforced the view that in the emerging new economic order both advanced and emerging countries have complementary roles to play. In order to achieve globally sustainable economic progress and stabilize the global financial system, they need to work synergistically.

Gaining a better understanding of the global and country specific economic development dynamics is important both for developing growth strategies and for creating a more stable financial system. Collecting relevant data at the global and country levels and analyzing them to arrive at actionable information aids us in gaining the necessary understanding. Often, it may be necessary to obtain data at industry and country levels.

Our world is an economically interconnected one, where many forces are at play and constantly changing. This requires efficient data gathering, analysis, and generation of actionable information. The stakeholders may include business corporations, nation states, economic development and research organizations, and investors.

Several global organizations, such as the World Bank, the IMF, the OECD, and leading consulting firms, such as McKinsey and PricewaterhouseCoopers, publish numerous research and survey reports that provide data and other qualitative information about the economy, trade, and topics relating to developed and emerging countries. In addition, various agencies release, at regular intervals, information relating to the comparative positions of various countries by metrics, such as the global competitiveness index, global innovation index, ease of doing business, nominal GDP, GDP growth rate, per capita income, export and import trade, demography, current account deficit, and others. While stakeholders have access to these metrics that provide macro data, they also require information and analysis specific to their needs. This is in fact one of our fortes at Marcus Goncalves Consulting Group (MGCG),* as such specific and nuanced international market research needs would require custom market research and further business intelligence analysis in order to refine the macro data and thus generate actionable information which supports the decision-making and related processes.

While the need for a research and analysis based approach in matters relating to economic growth and development requirements is well underway and open discussions are taking place in numerous multilateral forums, the same is not true about reforms in the global financial system. We believe the global financial system is still very much the prerogative of the few developed economies; especially the United States, with the dollar as the world's de facto currency, and continues to wield too much power. Regretfully, necessary informed discussions among monetary and other policy makers do not take place transparently. The growing disconnect between the financial economy and the underlying real economy is a source of serious concern that deserves the urgent attention of the policy makers, if a total collapse at some future date is to be averted. Presently, policy makers are in a quandary and seem quite content with putting out one crisis after the other.

True success of market research depends first on an unambiguous definition of the purpose of the exercise, accuracy of the research, timeliness of the data, and proper selection of the firm to carry out the market research and deep collaboration (i.e., partnership) between the involved parties or stakeholders.

Modern Global Economic Evolution and Industrialization

Industrialization, which started around 1780 in Europe and North America, changed the pace of the global economic evolution. While technological inventions and breakthroughs spurred growth of the manufacturing industry, trade among countries, and economic activities.

---

* www.mgcgusa.com

The global economic expansion resulted in the emergence of not only industrial centers of excellence and consumer demand centers, but also created markets for a broad portfolio of industrial products and goods that cater to basic needs and aspirational desires. Industrialization led to demand creation and fulfillment, increased consumption and investment, economic activity and wealth creation. It set in motion a virtuous cycle of economic expansion resulting in job creation in manufacturing industries and growth of institutions and support services, such as banking, finance, insurance, and transportation, that either center around industrialization or are offshoots.

Industrialization was an inflection point in human history, which forever transformed our lives. Inventions and technological developments, such as the steam engine and the creation of railroads, development of the internal combustion engine and the growth of the automotive industry, rapid expansion of information, and communication technology that began with the invention of vacuum tubes and have revolutionized mass transportation, personal mobility, personal and mass communication, and information processing and computing. Such developments have created livelihoods and opportunities outside the traditional vocations, initially in manufacturing and subsequently in service and financial sectors. This occurred first in Europe, the birthplace of industrialization, and thereafter, in North America. As industrialization progressed, some of these countries emerged as advanced economies of the modern era and became the home of large engineering and business conglomerates spanning manufacturing, infrastructure, healthcare, transportation, and banking.

Industrialization created a new wave of aspirational wants among people and the disposable incomes in their pockets empowered them to indulge in discretionary spending. This led to a virtuous cycle of demand creation and fulfillment, increased consumption and investment, and wealth creation, starting in the real economy and after in the financial economy. Bain & Company's report "A world awash in money" points out that while the rate of growth of world output of goods and services has seen an extended slowdown over recent decades, global financial assets have expanded at a rapid pace.[3]

Economic Growth Spreads to Asia

After incubating for decades in Europe and North America, industrialization spread to Japan and later to some other countries in East Asia, such as South Korea and Taiwan. While technological inventions and breakthroughs was the bedrock of economic growth in countries where industrialization took root, Japan took it to the next level though the path of productivity improvements by focusing on production processes, seen notably in automotive and electronic industries. Other countries in Asia, such as Singapore, South Korea, and Taiwan also latched onto the electronic and information technology industries' growth momentum to emerge as high-income economies during the latter half of the 20th century. Later, the opening up of China's economy and its integration into the global economy paved the way for it to emerge as the world's factory. The economic development is spreading to countries, such as India, Indonesia, and Vietnam. It may be interesting to note that three Asian countries China, Japan, and India, figure among the five largest economies of the world in terms of purchasing power parity (PPP) in the recent International Bank for Reconstruction and Development/The World Bank Report.*

The emerging economies' development spurred consumption demand outside the advanced markets for a wide range of manufactured industrial products. Manufacturing moved away from a monolithic structure to become collaborative entities; each entity focused on what it does best at locations nearby to consumption centers.

Typical examples of collaborative and deconstructed manufacturing are the electronic and information technology industries, which largely contributed to the growth of Asian countries, such as South Korea and Taiwan. Large conglomerates dominate this industry. While integrated device manufacturers, such as Intel and Samsung design, make, and sell

---

* Purchasing Power Parities and Real Expenditures of World Economies: Summary of Results and Findings of the 2011 International Comparison Program http://siteresources.worldbank.org/ICPINT/Resources/270056-1183395201801/Summary-of-Results-and-Findings-of-the-2011-International-Comparison-Program.pdf

their chips, fabless* manufacturers such as Qualcomm and AMD only design and sell chips by outsourcing manufacturing to foundry companies. While Sony and LG Electronics are among the leading suppliers of consumer electronic goods, Lenovo and HP are top suppliers of personal computers. These companies then buy embedded devices from vendors such as Texas Instruments, and they in turn depend on companies such as Wipro and HCL Technologies to develop embedded software.

Companies such as Microsoft and SAP dominate the software market. Many of these companies and their affiliates have facilities in geographically dispersed locations. The expansion of the electronics industry, of which information and communication technology is comprised, not only helped countries in Asia to prosper but also resulted in increasing intra-regional and inter-regional trade. In the Working Paper,[4] "Fragmentation and East Asia's Information Technology Trade" published in 2004, the authors Carl Bonham, Byron Gangnes, and Ari Van Assche argued, "Over the past two decades, international production fragmentation by U.S. and Japanese IT firms has gradually turned developing East Asia into a global manufacturing base for IT products." On one hand, this provided further impetus for the economic growth across countries in Asia, especially in ASEAN countries, and on the other to the consolidation of globalization trends. Countries and companies that successfully align their growth strategies with global trends reap the benefits.

New Economic Order and Financial System Vulnerabilities

When economic growth began to spread across countries in East and South East Asia, by mid-1990s the Japanese economy began to show signs of slowdown, driven by various factors including U.S. pressure. Later, loss of trade due to the emergence of China as a low cost manufacturer and demographic influence on the country's labor further accentuated the situation. In addition, Japan also experienced an asset price bubble resulting ing stock and asset prices. Since then, Japan has not been successful in reviving its growth, and in 2010 the country ceded its moniker

---

con wafer manufacturing facilities.

as the world' second largest economy to China. The recent International Bank for Reconstruction and Development/The World Bank Report* says that India has displaced Japan to emerge as the world's third largest economy in terms of purchasing power parity (PPP). India moved from 10th place 2005 to 3rd place in 2011.

It may be safe to hypothesize that Japan's protracted slowdown is among the first indicator of two developments; one, the emergence of a new economic order in the shaping of which emerging markets would play a significant role and two, the vulnerability of the global financial system.

Figure 2.1 shows how the Chinese economy has overtaken the advanced economies of France, UK, Germany, and Japan, and how the Japanese economy remained stagnant for well over a decade while China was expanding.

Due to increased economic development in emerging countries, the world is witnessing the emergence of a massive middleclass population with significant disposable incomes and a robust appetite for aspirational wants, such as automobiles and consumer durables. If their demands are to be satisfied, these countries need a robust manufacturing industry, which many lack. Typically, emerging countries continue to struggle in overcoming the initial mover advantage that advanced countries continue to enjoy in the industrial sector. However, a few have grasped the technology, acquired the negotiating power due to their recent achievement of economic growth, and emerged attractive to would be global investors.

The importance of the manufacturing industry in spurring growth in emerging countries cannot be overstated. A McKinsey report[5] "Manufacturing the growth: The next era of global growth" says very aptly "… manufacturing remains critically important to both the developing and the advanced world. In the former, it continues to provide a pathway from subsistence agriculture to rising incomes and living standards. In the latter, it remains a vital source of innovation and competitiveness,

---

* Purchasing Power Parities and Real Expenditures of World Economies: Summary of Results and Findings of the 2011 International Comparison Program http://siteresources.worldbank.org/ICPINT/Resources/270056-1183395201801/Summary-of-Results-and-Findings-of-the-2011-International-Comparison-Program.pdf

(a)

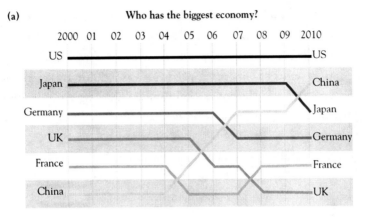

(b)

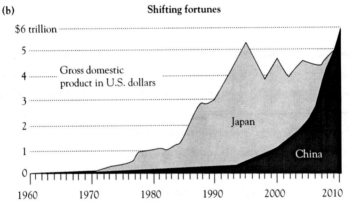

Figure 2.1 China's economy has overtaken France, UK, Germany, and Japan, the advanced economies

Source: The World Bank; IMF

making outsized contributions to research and development, exports, and productivity growth." It is important to add that sustainable growth is possible *only when* all other industries work together in supporting the framework, including the service industry, banking and finance, law and a national policy on taxation and trade. As economic prosperity expands, the aspirational demand for services increases and the service industry expands. In their book,[6] "Beyond Economic Growth," authors Tatyana P. Soubbotina with Katherine A. Sheram, underscore this thought; "As incomes continue to rise, people's needs become less 'material' and they begin to demand more services—in health, education, entertainment, and many other areas."

Resulting from the spread of industrialization and wealth creation, we are witnessing the emergence of new economic order in which emerging countries would play an important role. The formal recognition by the G7 countries, discussed in earlier chapters, verifies that close integration of their economies with emerging countries and effective collaboration with them is necessary to sustain the long-term global economic growth strategies, and led to the creation of G-20.

Despite the exclusion of some large economies, G-20 acts as an excellent platform to deliberate and decide on mutually beneficial economic growth and financial strategies. Of course, advanced and emerging countries have other platforms, such as trade agreements and groupings like Transatlantic Trade and Investment Partnership (TTIP) and Association of Southeast Asian Nations (ASEAN) in which to achieve national and regional economic objectives.

The scope of G20's deliberations includes, apart from economic growth and globalization issues, matters relating to the international financial system. The U.S. subprime mortgage crisis in 2008, the banking crisis in Ireland and the European sovereign debt crisis, which began in 2009, have brought to the fore front the weaknesses in the financial system. Figure 2.2 illustrates the global capital pyramid and the magnitude of its impact on global GDP growth.

Figure 2.2 A $27 trillion growth in global GDP will support a $300 trillion increase in total financial assets by 2020

Source: IMF; OECD; Bain

As depicted in Figure 2.2, with the current financial assets at nearly 10 times the value of the global output of all goods and services,[7] the relationship between the financial economy and the underlying real economy has become unformulated and unstable. The financial assets, subjected to speculative forces, keep expanding. While getting divorced from the real economy of the common people, who constitute the majority, the expanding financial economy is beginning to affect them profoundly. It accentuates the normal business growth and downturn cycles, creates asset bubbles, and leads to currency fluctuations. Resulting from the financial economy's growing disconnect with the real economy it has reached a decisive point which calls for the financial market participants and other policy makers to initiate corrective measures.

While discussions relating to the role of emerging countries in ensuring sustainable global economic growth and global trade continue to make progress, discussions on the appropriate steps for ensuring the stability of the financial system have not. In order to move forward, stakeholders must make serious efforts to address the core issues instead of short-term fixes.

Market Research Imperatives for Success in Emerging Markets

Emerging markets are key partners to advanced economies because they have evolved both as consumption and production centers and thereby play an important role as global economic growth engines. By 2025, consumers in emerging-markets will spend almost $30 trillion annually, up from $12 trillion today.* Thus, the growing middle-class in emerging economies represents new markets for advanced countries and their multinational corporations. While advanced economies have surplus capital and technology, emerging countries are low-cost economies, but with easy availability of skilled human resources. Consequently, emerging countries are target markets, manufacturing bases, and sourcing destinations for advanced economies and their multinational corporations.

---

* http://www.mckinsey.com/insights/winning_in_emerging_markets/winning_the_30_trillion_decathlon_how_to_succeed_in_emerging_markets

While emerging markets offer excellent growth opportunities, only companies which invest in understanding the country-specific market information and enter the market with appropriate strategies that help them to align with the nuances of the market, can hope to emerge successful. Succeeding in an emerging market is not easy, but the market opportunities are too attractive to be ignored. The McKinsey report "Winning the $30 Trillion Decathlon: Going for gold in Emerging markets" points out that in 2010, 100 of the world's largest companies headquartered in developed economies derived just 17 percent of their total revenue from emerging markets—though those markets accounted for 36 percent of global GDP. This situation highlights the challenges of emerging markets.

Companies strategizing to enter the emerging markets must acknowledge, on one hand, that these markets operate under distinct business models and structures and on the other invest in gaining on-the-ground knowledge. Through in-depth market research, they must gain a good understanding the market and the political, economic, and business environments. They must structure the market research to obtain information relating to the market size and growth potential, competitive landscape, customers' preferences, overall economic and political outlook, skill availability, legal and taxation environment, and others. A manufacturing company must additionally gather details regarding issues relating to supply chain such as the availability of raw materials and components, logistics, distribution channels, and more.

In Chapter 1, we have examined some of the important issues about which a company must have a deep understanding to successfully do business in an emerging market. Some of the important information required includes details relating to the availability of support infrastructures and institutions in the emerging market that multinational corporations take for granted.

Companies entering an emerging market must have a good understanding of the country's political and economic outlook so that they are not caught off guard. Some of the emerging countries are experiencing serious political unrests that may lead to economic instability. Additionally, many of the emerging economies frequently change tax laws, place import restrictions, impose foreign exchange controls, resort to price controls, among others. Emerging markets also may lack the transparency that companies in advanced economies are used to. We have discussed some of the related issues in Chapters 3 and 4. Companies must regularly evaluate and assess these risks and track developments in these areas.

Yet another area of concern for companies interested in the emerging markets is the possible destabilizing impact on them and when the advanced economies begin to withdraw from their easy money policies. This can trigger potentially massive reversal of capital flows and result in currency fluctuations. Chapter 5 discusses some of the issues relating to this aspect. Companies entering the emerging markets must investigate to gain necessary insights and develop counter measures to protect their interests.

Market Research, Business Intelligence, and Actionable Information

Numerous global organizations, such as World Bank, the OECD, and leading consulting firms such as McKinsey and Boston Consulting develop research and survey reports that provide data and qualitative information about the global economy, industry, and topics relating to advanced and emerging countries. In addition, various agencies release at regular intervals information relating the comparative position of countries by metrics, such as ease of doing business, global competitiveness index, nominal GDP, GDP growth rate, per capita income, export and import trade, demography, current account deficit, and global innovation index.

Stakeholders, such as the business corporations, nation states, consultants and analyst firms, institutional and private equity investors, and economic development and research organizations interested in global economic development and in ensuring the future stability of the financial system, need not only macro level data and basic information but they need it in granular detail.

The speed of change is increasing at an amazing rate throughout emerging and frontier markets. To prepare for accelerated change in such markets, multinational companies need to look at five critical factors in order to have a higher rate of success when entering such markets: social, technological, environmental, economic, and political. In addition, the management team must engage these drivers of change seriously, by asking themselves and the leadership how to develop a "fierce strategy" to compete abroad, one that can be disruptive to the local market and industry. This way of thinking and strategy development sets the stage for actions management can take to benefit from, rather than be overwhelmed by, this rapidly changing environment in such markets.

With the help of analytics, business intelligence, and modeling and simulation tools they can, from market research reports, generate actionable information that help them make informed decisions. Business intelligence and modeling and simulation tools also could help them to perform what-if analyses under changing economic scenarios and study futuristic scenarios.

Succeeding in business, formulating a country's growth strategies, making the right investment decisions, developing and introducing the right product, and advising clients about business transformation are complex and require real time information gathering and analysis with powerful algorithms.

Qualitative and quantitative information gathering or market research, both primary and secondary, is required to identify market needs, opportunities, and threats, to make informed decisions. It is the minimum required to maximize the probability of success and minimizes risks. The type of information required would depend on the stakeholder's specific needs. For example, an automotive company from a developed country, interested in establishing its business presence in an emerging country, might like to research for information, such as the country's demand projection, growth prospects, competitors profile, import policy and tariffs, acceptable price points, buying pattern, and business nuances. Its initial interest may be to shortlist few countries out of list of probable countries that have business potential and a high probability of success.

In order to select the country or countries, the company would invariably need information, such as the country's market size, GDP, and per capita income growth rates, demography, import–export trade, currency rate, economic, and political stability. The required information is customized to the stakeholder's needs and the information gathered is country and timeframe specific. After deciding upon the country in which to expand, the company may shift its focus to select potential partners, necessitating operational, financial, and legalese requiring extensive detailed data gathering and information analysis. After establishing a presence, the company might like to have research about brand acceptance, customer satisfaction, its market share, and prospects of launching a new product into the market. On the other hand, a developed country's automotive industry association, wanting to estimate the business potential for its members might require more broad based market research to gather information, such as current status of the industry, demand patterns and growth potential for compact cars, trucks, sport utility vehicles, and sedans in selected countries.

If, instead of the automotive company, a consumer durable manufacturer from a developed country wanted to explore the feasibility of entering an emerging market, the research requirements would be very different. Typically, a consumer durable manufacturer would be offering a broad portfolio of products ranging from simple generic models to feature-rich high-end products. Therefore, the company may need information that would facilitate decision making on matters relating to sales channels, which products to offer initially, branding strategy, distribution logistics, and best location of the company's production facility.

On the other hand, if a developing country wants to draw up the country's industrial roadmap, it would probably start by researching the country's developmental needs and priorities, its industry's capacity to absorb the technology, and skill availability.

The need for research-based data and information gathering and the use of analytics, business intelligence, and modeling and simulation tools to analyze and generate actionable information to track the efficacy of the actions is that much greater in a world on the threshold of entering a new economic order. The lingering perception is that organizations and institutions operating in the realm of a real economy more often resort to a research and analytical based approach in comparison to those belonging to the financial economic fraternity.

While the capturing of accurate qualitative and quantitative information is important. Stakeholders must also clearly define upfront the purpose of the exercise, as that will decide the research methodology and the information to be gathered and analyzed. They must be clear in stipulating what data and information they need it, why they need it, and how they intend to use it. The answers to these questions would determine the type, either primary or secondary, and in the case of primary, the questionnaire design, mode of data and information collection, and the responsible agency. In the case of secondary research, the sources, their time relevance, and reliability would be important. Market research requires that it be both systematic and objective to serve the intended purpose. Prior to analyzing the data and information, it is necessary to validate it.

Selecting and appointing the firm to carry out the market research plays a crucial role in a project's success. This process involves evaluating the past performance of the market research firm and assessing whether it has the necessary resources, such as the required field staff, domain knowledge, and the expertise. It is important for the stakeholder commissioning the market research, to be completely involved during each phases of the market research, such as formulating the questionnaire and the data, and information gathering methodology.

CHAPTER 3

Coping With Political and Economic Risks

Overview

Diversification in global trading benefits international business investments, especially in emerging markets, which have become a prominent feature of the financial globalization sweeping the world over the last decade. Whether conducting business or investing in emerging markets, corporations and investors are always exposed to political environments that are not typically present in advanced economies.

The risk of major violence is greatest when high levels of stress combine with weak and illegitimate national institutions. Emerging nations are vulnerable when their institutions are unable to protect their citizens from abuse, or to provide equitable access to justice and economic opportunity. These vulnerabilities are exacerbated in countries with high youth unemployment, growing income inequality, and perceptible injustice. In addition, externally driven events such as infiltration by foreign combatants, the presence of trafficking networks, or economic shocks add to the stresses that can provoke violence.

According to the World Bank's World Development Report 2011, about 1.5 billion people live in countries affected by repeated cycles of political and criminal violence, and no low-income fragile or conflict-affected country has yet to achieve a single Millennium Development Goal.* Fixing the economic, political, and security problems that disrupt development and trap fragile states in cycles of violence requires

---

* The Millennium Development Goals (MDGs) are eight international development goals that were established following the Millennium Summit of the United Nations in 2000, following the adoption of the United Nations Millennium Declaration.

strengthening national institutions and improving governance in ways that prioritize citizen security, justice, and jobs.

Political and economic risks in emerging and frontier markets, apart from the very human cost of fragility, influence international business development, foreign trade, and foreign investors' perceptions of risk, especially political risk, which affects private sector activity. This produces a vicious cycle, where these economies worsen, increasingly fragility, especially in frontier markets. By frontier markets we mean the type of country that is not yet a developed market. The term is an economic term coined by International Finance Corporation's (IFC) Farida Khambata in 1992. The term is used commonly to describe the equity markets of the smaller and less accessible, but still "investable," countries of the developing world. These countries were in the past emerging markets. For more in-depth information, please refer to our book, *Comparing Emerging and Advanced Markets: Current Trends and Challenges,* same publisher, which provides much more breadth and depth on the topic.

Coping with Risks

Over the past two decades, we have witnessed Russian default on its debt to foreigners in 1998, the Mexican peso crisis in 1994, and the Asian economic meltdown in 1997. While these risks are usually well known to major banks and multinational companies, and assessment techniques in these domains are relatively well developed, they tend not to be appropriate in assessing the geopolitical aspects associated with cross country correlations.

Political risks for foreign direct investments (FDI) are affected when difficult to anticipate discontinuities resulting from political change occur in the international business environment. Some example include the potential restrictions on the transfer of funds, products, technology and people, uncertainty about policies, regulations, governmental administrative procedures, and risks on control of capital such as discrimination against foreign firms, expropriation, forced local shareholding, and so on. Wars, revolutions, social upheavals, strikes, economic growth, inflation, and exchange rates should be figured into the political and economic risk assessment, as these instances can negatively impact local investments as well as FDI.

Recent Political Unrests

Slowing economies, oppressive regimes, and broad societal changes have contributed to political instability in emerging markets and other countries in recent years. Corporations and international business professionals with interests in such areas face the potential for political violence, terrorist attacks, resource nationalism, and expropriation actions that can jeopardize the safety and security of their people, assets, and supply chains.

risks that —

Conducting business internationally, therefore, may offer many opportunities, but not without risks, especially political ones. There have been a myriad of events occurring around the world in the past three years, particularly among emerging economies, more notably the MENA region, as depicted in Figure 3.1.

The Arab Spring *affected so many countries*

The Arab Spring, a revolutionary wave of demonstrations and protests, riots, and civil wars in the Arab world, began in early December 2010. Its effects are still lingering. As of November 2013 rulers from this region have been forced from power, as in Tunisia,[1] which took down the

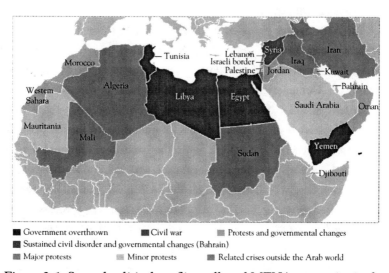

Government overthrown   ■ Civil war   ■ Protests and governmental changes
■ Sustained civil disorder and governmental changes (Bahrain)
■ Major protests   ■ Minor protests   ■ Related crises outside the Arab world

Figure 3.1 Several political conflicts affected MENA economies in the past three years

politically + economically (list all)

country's long-time dictator, Zine El Abidine Ben Ali. At the time, many were looking to it as a turning point for the Arab world, and rampant speculation begun about what it could mean for other countries toiling under Islamic dictatorships.

Many Arab Spring demonstrations have been met with violent responses from authorities, as well as from pro-government militias and counter-demonstrators. These attacks have been answered with violence from protestors in some cases. A major slogan of the demonstrators in the Arab world has been *Ash-sha`b yurid isqat an-nizam* ("the people want to bring down the regime").[2] Hence, at the same time Tunisia, Egypt and Libya were dealing with the consequences of the Arab Spring, civil uprisings were also breaking out in Bahrain and Syria, while several major protests continued to erupt in Algeria, Iraq, Jordan, Kuwait, Morocco, and Sudan.

Tunisia, Where the Arab Spring Began

The Arab Spring started in Tunisia. The country's "Jasmine Revolution" was the first popular uprising to topple an established government in the Middle East and North Africa since the Iranian revolution of 1979. The revolution in Tunisia also was the spark that ignited and inspired other revolutions in the region.

The Arab Spring unfolded in three phases. First, on December 17, 2011, a young Tunisian street vendor, Mohamed Bouazizi, set himself on fire in hopelessness and to protest his treatment at the hands of the authorities. Demonstrations broke out in his rural hometown followed by protests in other areas of the country. A brutal security crackdown followed, reported in chocking details by online social media. Second, when protests reached the capital, Tunis, the government responded with even more brutality, arresting demonstrators, activists, and shutting down the Internet. Lastly, President Zine el-Abedin Ben Ali shuffled his cabinet and promised to create 300,000 jobs, but it was too late; protesters now just wanted the regime to fall and its President stripped of any power. On January 14, Ben Ali and his family fled the country taking refuge in Saudi Arabia. This act marked the end of one of the Arab world's most repressive regimes. It was a victory for people power and perhaps the first time ever in history that an Arab dictator has been removed by a revolution rather than a coup d'Etat.

Egypt

Although the Arab Spring began in Tunisia, the decisive moment that changed the Arab region forever was the downfall of Egyptian President Hosni Mubarak, ensconced in power since 1980. Similar to Tunisia, mass protests started in late January of 2011 and by early February, Mubarak was forced to resign after the military refused to intervene against the masses occupying Tahrir Square in Cairo.

Deep divisions emerged over the new political system as Islamists from the Freedom and Justice Party (FJP) won the parliamentary and presidential election in 2011 and 2012, thus souring relations with secular parties who continued protests for deeper political change. The Egyptian military remains the single most powerful political player, and much of the old regime remains in place. The economy has been in decline since the start of unrest.[3] By the time Mubarak resigned, large portions of the Middle East were already in turmoil. While the Egyptian people succeeded in overthrowing Mubarak from power, the Supreme Council of Armed Forces (SCAF) continues to run the country in a transition period marked by violence and instability.

At the time of these writings, June 2014, a veteran politician, Ibrahim Mahlab, who was serving as Egypt's interim prime minister. He was sworn in as the head of a new cabinet by President Abdel Fattah el-Sisi in the president's first major decision since his election victory in May 2014. Sisi has promised to restore security and the country's struggling economy at the top of his agenda, and has pledged to build a more stable future after three turbulent years since the toppling of longtime ruler Hosni Mubarak.

Libya

Soon after Mubarak's resignation, in February 2011, protests against Col. Muammar al-Qaddafi's regime in Libya started in front of Benghazi's police headquarters following the arrest of a human rights attorney who represented the "relatives of more than 1,000 prisoners allegedly massacred by security forces in Tripoli's Abu Salim jail in 1996," which escalated into the first civil war caused by the Arab Spring.

What began as a series of peaceful demonstrations turned into confrontations, which were met with military force. When the National Conference for the Libyan Opposition organized a "Day of Rage" (February 17, 2011), the Libyan military and security forces did not allowed the demonstration to go on and fired live ammunition on protesters. The following day, security forces withdrew from Benghazi after being overwhelmed by protesters, while some security personnel also joined the protesters. The protests spread across the country and anti-Gaddafi forces established a provisional government based in Benghazi, called the National Transitional Council with the stated goal to overthrow the Gaddafi government in Tripoli.

NATO* forces had to intervene in March 2011 against Qaddafi's army helping the opposition rebel movement capture most of the country by August 2011. In October 2011 Qaddafi was killed, but the rebels' coup was short-lived, as various rebel militias effectively partitioned the country among them, leaving a weak central government that continues to struggle to exert its authority and provide basic services to its citizens. Most of the oil production has returned on stream, but political violence remains endemic, and religious extremism has been on the rise.[4]

Yemen

Even before the Arab Spring from Tunisia and Egypt reached Yemen, President Saleh's regime faced daunting challenges. In the north, it was battling the Huthi rebellion. In the south it faced an ever-growing secessionist movement. Al-Qaeda in the Arabian Peninsula was showing mounting signs of activism. Sanaa's political class was locked in a two-year battle over electoral and constitutional reforms while behind the scenes a fierce competition for post-Saleh spoils was underway. Economic conditions for the average Yemenis were dismal and worsening.

---

* North Atlantic Treaty Organization, an international organization composed of the U.S., Canada, UK, and a number of European countries for purposes of collective security.

Bolstered by events in Tunisia, anti-government protesters of all political parties started pouring onto the streets in mid-January 2011. Hundreds of people died in clashes as pro-government forces organized rival rallies, and the army began to disintegrate into two political camps.

Largely caught off guard, the regime's response was mixed. It employed harsh tactics, particularly in the south, arresting, beating, harassing, and even killing activists. By most accounts, regime supporters donning civilian clothes took the lead, wielding sticks, clubs, knives, and guns to disperse demonstrations. Police and security personnel at best failed to protect protesters, at worst encouraged or even participated in the repression. On March 8, 2011 the army used live ammunition against demonstrators and represented a worrisome escalation.

Still, Yemen was neither Egypt nor Tunisia. Notwithstanding, Egypt was not like Tunisia, which says something about how oblivious popular protests are to societal differences and how idle speculations can be regarding what a regime might do next. Yemen's regime was less repressive, more broadly inclusive and adaptable. It appeared to have perfected the art of co-opting its opposition, and as a result, the extensive patronage network discouraged many from directly challenging the president. Moreover, flawed as they are, the country had, and still has, working institutions, including a multi-party system, a parliament, and local government.

Nonetheless, the protesters, with the wind at their backs, expected nothing less than the president's quick ouster. The president and those who have long benefited from his rule were not willing to give in without a fight. Finding a compromise was nearly impossible as the regime would have to make significant concessions, indeed far more extensive than it so far had been willing to do. To be meaningful, these concessions would have to have touched the core of a political system that had relied on patron-client networks and on the military-security apparatus. Besides, a democratic transition was long overdue.

As a result, in the end, the Yemeni leader Ali Abdullah Saleh became the fourth victim of the Arab Spring. Amidst this turmoil, Al Qaeda in Yemen began to seize territory in the south of the country. Had it not been for Saudi Arabia's facilitation of a political settlement Yemen would have fallen victim to an all-out civil war. President Saleh signed the transition deal on November 23, 2011, agreeing to step aside for a transitional government led by the Vice-President Abd al-Rab Mansur al-Hadi. How-ever, little progress toward a stable democratic order has been made and regular Al Qaeda attacks, separatism in the south, tribal disputes, and a collapsing economy are all stalling this nascent transition.[5]

Protests in Bahrain

Protests in Bahrain began on February 2012, just days after Mubarak's resignation. Bahrain has always had a long history of tension between the ruling Sunni royal family, and the majority Shiite population demanding greater political and economic rights. The Arab Spring acted as a catalyst, reenergizing the largely Shiite protest movement, driving tens of thou-sands to the streets defying fire from security forces. The Bahraini royal family was saved by a military intervention of neighboring countries led by Saudi Arabia. A political solution, however, was not reached and the crackdown failed to suppress the protest movement. As of early fall 2013, protests, clashes with security forces, and arrests of opposition activists continue in that country with no solution in sight.[6]

More recently (March 2014), tensions between Qatar and neighbor-ing Persian Gulf monarchies broke out when Saudi Arabia, the United Arab Emirates and Bahrain withdrew their ambassadors from the country over its support of the Muslim Brotherhood* and allied Islamists around the region. The concerted effort to isolate Qatar, a tiny, petroleum-rich peninsula, was an extraordinary rebuke of its strategy of aligning with moderate Islamists in the hope of extending its influence amid the Arab Spring revolts.

But in recent months Islamists' gains have been rolled back, with the military takeover in Egypt, the governing party shaken in Turkey, chaos in Libya, and military gains by the government in Syria. The other gulf monarchies always had bridled at Qatar's tactic, viewing popular demands for democracy and political Islam as dual threats to their power.

---

* The Muslim Brotherhood is a multi-national Islamic revivalist organization based in Egypt and founded by a primary school teacher, Hassan al-Banna. Origi-nally established in 1928 as a social youth club stressing moral and social reform rooted in Islam, by 1939 it had turned into a political organization.

The Saudi monarchs, in particular, have grumbled for years as tiny Qatar has swaggered around like a heavyweight. It used its huge wealth and Al Jazeera, which it owns, as instruments of regional power. It negotiated a peace deal in Lebanon, supported Palestinian militants in Gaza, shipped weapons to rebels in Libya and Syria, and gave refuge to exiled leaders of Egypt's Brotherhood; all while certain its own security was assured by the presence of a major American military base.

Conflicts in Syria

Syria, a multi-religious country allied with Iran, ruled by a repressive republican regime, and amid a pivotal geo-political position was next. The major protests began in March 2011 in provincial towns at first, but gradually spreading to all major urban areas. The regime's brutality provoked an armed response from the opposition, and by mid-2011 Army defectors began organizing in the Free Syrian Army.

Consequently, by the end of 2011, Syria descended into civil war as rebel brigades battled government forces for control of cities, towns, and the countryside. Fighting reached the capital Damascus and second city of Aleppo in 2012. This war is still ongoing today, with most of the Alawite* religious minority siding with President Bashar al-Assad, and most of the Sunni majority supporting the rebels. Both camps have outside backers. Russia supports the regime. Saudi Arabia supports the rebels. Neither side is able to break the deadlock.[7]

The armed rebellion has evolved significantly, with as many as 1,000 groups commanding an estimated 100,000 fighters. Secular moderates are outnumbered by Islamists and jihadists linked to al-Qaeda, whose brutal tactics have caused widespread concern and triggered rebel infighting. Although investigators have been denied entry into Syria and their communications with witnesses have been restricted, investigators have confirmed at least 27 incidents of intentional mass killings.

In July 2013, as depicted in Figure 3.2, the UN said more than 100,000 people had been killed. It has stopped updating the death toll,

---

* Member of a Shiite Muslim group living mainly in Syria.

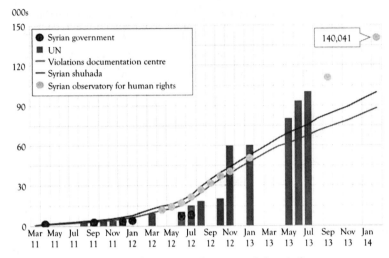

Figure 3.2 Syrian casualties since the start of the civil war

Source: UN

but activists say it now exceeds 140,000. According to BBC,* a UN commission of inquiry has been investigating all alleged violations of international human rights law since March 2011. It has evidence showing that both sides have committed war crimes including torture, hostage taking, murder, and execution. The commission argues that 17 of these war crimes were perpetrated by government forces and pro-government militia, including incidents that left hundreds of civilians dead in Houla in May 2012 and Baniyas in August 2013. Rebel groups have been blamed for 10 massacres, including the slaughter of at least 190 people in the Latakia countryside in August 2013 by jihadist and hardline Islamist fighters.

Conflicts in Morocco

On February 20, 2011, the Arab Spring engulfed Morocco, when thousands of protesters gathered in the capital city of Rabat. They demanded greater social justice and limits to King Mohammed VI's power. The king responded by offering constitutional amendments ceding some of his

---

* http://www.bbc.com/news/world-middle-east-26116868

powers, and by calling a fresh parliamentary election that was controlled less by the royal court than in previous elections.

The message of a democratic agenda and gradual change was one that has gone down well with Morocco's allies in the United States and Europe. We believe the Arab World is in the process of changing. It is still too soon to prognostic the results of which political and socioeconomic direction Egypt, Tunisia, Syria, or Yemen will take. We also believe that if there is a country impacted by the Arab Spring that may become an example on how to bring about a gentle revolution that could eventually become a real democracy, that is Morocco. How long it will take and if it ever will happen is anyone's guess, as the reforms passed in 2011 are still largely cosmetic and there is no guarantee they will be put into practice on the ground.

The king retains ultimate control and though parliament has more power, the political parties are weak. These reforms, coupled with fresh state funds to help low-income families, diminished the appeal of the protest movement, with many Moroccans content with the king's program of gradual reform. Rallies demanding a genuine constitutional monarchy continue, but have so far failed to mobilize the masses as it did in Tunisia and Egypt.[8]

Demonstrations in Jordan

Demonstrations in Jordan gained momentum in late January 2011, as Islamists, leftist groups and youth activists protested against living conditions and corruption. Parallel to Morocco, most Jordanians wanted reform, rather than abolish the monarchy, giving King Abdullah II the breathing space his republican counterparts in other Arab countries didn't have. Consequently, the king managed to ease the Arab Spring by making superficial changes to the political system and reorganizing the government. Fear of chaos similar to Syria did the rest. To date, the economy, however, is still performing poorly and none of the key issues have been addressed, which may prompt protesters' demands to grow more radical over time.[9]

Jordan's version of the Arab Spring may have been over quietly and unceremoniously, but regional upheavals, especially in Syria and Egypt, have dampened Jordanians' appetite for drastic change in their own country. Back in 2012, tens of anti-government protests took place in Jordan, especially on Fridays. The Muslim Brotherhood organized most of them, but the Jordanian Youth Movement, or hirak, whose slogans often crossed red lines, led some. They called for regime change and accused King Abdullah II of corruption. Many of their leaders are now in prison and some will stand trial in front of the State Security Court (SSC) on charges that range from insulting the king to attempting to overthrow the regime.

Although it has been a few years since the large demonstrations were held in Amman or elsewhere, back in November 2012, when the newly appointed government of Abdullah Ensour floated the price of gasoline and ended state subsidies, thousands took to the streets and the country saw three days of angry demonstrations and clashes with the police. The opposition, an alliance between the Islamists and a coalition of leftist and nationalist groups and parties called the National Reform Front (NRF), threatened to further derail austerity measures. When the government raised the price of electricity last month nothing happened. It was a sign that neither the Islamists nor the rest of the opposition were able to mobilize the street anymore.

Despite worsening economic conditions Jordanians became wary of instability and chaos that gripped neighboring Syria and Egypt, and indeed, most Arab Spring countries. Stability and security became more important than pressing for immediate political reforms. A growing number of Jordanians became suspicious of the Muslim Brotherhood agenda for Jordan. In fact, the alliance between the Islamists and NRF quickly unraveled when a prominent Brotherhood leader insisted that the goal of the movement was to establish a Sharia-led Islamic state in Jordan.

Regional changes have allowed the regime to recalibrate its position on issues. King Abdullah successfully weathered the storm by avoiding the use of violence and presenting himself as a champion of reforms. In 2012, he introduced important constitutional amendments and created a constitutional court. He published a number of papers on his vision for a democratic transition. While the controversial elections law was altered slightly, he organized legislative elections in early 2013 and introduced the first parliamentary government, which he said should remain in office for the entire term of the four-year Lower House.

We believe, however, that it may be too soon to assume the Jordanian's Arab Spring is over. Economic challenges remain dire even as Gulf countries and the United States continue to pump money into Jordan's coffers. Unemployment and poverty rates are still very high and the country has seen the worst episodes of societal violence in decades. As of spring of 2014, more than half a million Syrian refugees in Jordan have added unexpected burdens on the local economy. Political life has stagnated and people's approval of parliament has plummeted. A recent incident when a Kalashnikov*-toting deputy tried to kill a colleague has renewed debate about the need to amend the election law and breathe life into political parties.

Furthermore, the Jordanian government is still unpopular, and unless economic life improves soon, we believe Jordanians may go back to the street in protest. The majority of protests that take place these days are economic in nature. In addition, the king has evaded substantial political reforms that relate to the complex issues of Jordanian identity and his own prerogatives as monarch; a major challenge in a country where at least half of its citizens are of Palestinian origin. The vital question now is how long can he ignore such issues?

So far he has been able to prove that Jordan is the exception to the rule in the Arab Spring saga, a similar situation experienced by Morocco. Jordan has avoided a repetition of the Egyptian or Syrian scenarios. The king has overcome popular protests and was able to repulse Muslim Brotherhood pressures. Jordanians are in no mood to take to the streets now, but that situation could change at any time.

Algeria

Algerian protests, which started in late December 2010, were inspired by similar protests across the MENA region. Causes cited include unemployment, the lack of housing, food-price inflation, corruption, restrictions on freedom of speech, and poor living conditions. While localized protests were already commonplace over previous years, extending into

---

* A type of rifle or submachine gun made in Russia, especially the AK-47 assault rifle.

December 2010, an unprecedented wave of simultaneous protests and riots sparked by sudden rises in staple food prices erupted all over the country beginning in January 2011.

These protests were suppressed by government swiftly lowering food prices, but were followed by a wave of self-immolations, most of which occurred in front of government buildings. Despite being illegal to do so without government permission, opposition parties, unions and human rights groups began holding weekly demonstrations. The government's reaction was swift repression of these demonstrations.[10]

In our research, we found that many nationals who experienced the Arab Spring would have preferred it never happened. Think of the mayhem that would have been avoided in Egypt and Syria, not to mention Libya, Yemen, and Bahrain, where the angry and the aggrieved have created chaos in the name of democracy. How foolish of advanced economies of the West, especially the United States and UK to turn on allies like Hosni Mubarak, and to pander to the Muslim Brotherhood, while assorting to narrow-minded Islamists. Unless of course, it was done on purpose.

Iraq

The 2011 Iraqi protests came in the wake of the Tunisian and Egyptian revolutions. The protests resulted in at least 45 deaths, including at least 29 on the *Day of Rage*, which took place on February 25, 2011. Several of the protests in March 2011, however, were against the Saudi-led intervention in Bahrain.[11]

Protests also took place in Iraqi Kurdistan, an autonomous Kurdish region in Iraq's north that lasted for 62 consecutive days. More recently, on December 21, 2012, a group raided Sunni Finance Minister Rafi al-Issawi's home and resulted in the arrest of 10 of his bodyguards.[12] Beginning in Fallujah, the protests have since spread throughout Sunni Arab parts of Iraq, and have even gained support from non-Sunni Iraqi politicians, such as Muqtada al-Sadr. Pro-Maliki protests have taken place throughout southern Iraq, where there is a Shia Arab majority. In April 2013, sectarian violence escalated after the 2013 Hawija clashes.[13]

Kuwait

Kuwaiti protests took place in 2011–2012, also calling for government reforms. On November 28, 2011, the government of Kuwait resigned in response to the protests, making Kuwait one of several countries affected by the Arab Spring to experience major governmental changes due to unrest.[14]

In early April 2014, however, Kuwait's once-feisty opposition appeared waning. Protests that in 2012 brought tens of thousands to the streets to call for reform had fizzled out while personality conflicts splintered a broad coalition of youth, Islamists, leftists, and tribal figures. Pundits declared Kuwait's never-quite-Arab spring a bust.

But the public waning act masked what may be the most intense scheming in Kuwait in a decade. On April 12, 2014, Kuwait's opposition re-emerged with a new website, politburo, media operation, and most importantly, demand for full parliamentary democracy. It is the most ambitious reform recently proposed in the Gulf, where Kuwait is the most democratic of all the monarchies.

The call for change is likely to send jitters across the rest of the Gulf, where Kuwait is used as a symbol of why democracy is a bad idea. Fighting between Kuwait's parliament and cabinet (the latter is named by the emir) have held up key infrastructure projects, caused instability, and diminished public confidence. But if Kuwait can surmount those obstacles and gives its people a greater say in their country, it will become a source of fear.

Sudan

As part of the Arab Spring, protests in Sudan began in January 2011 with a regional protest movement. Unlike other Arab countries, however, popular uprisings in Sudan succeeded in toppling the government prior to the Arab Spring, in both 1964 and 1985. Demonstrations were less common throughout the summer of 2011, during which time South Sudan seceded from Sudan. It resumed in force in June 2012 shortly after the government passed its much criticized austerity plan.[15]

The Sudanese government, however, has absorbed the second shock triggered by its decision to remove fuel subsidies. This shock was even more violent than the first that hit the country in 2012. Yet Sudan is likely to face a third shock in 2014, which may be as violent and bloody as the recent wave of protests. This will occur when the government completely lifts fuel subsidies, which will increase the prices of many goods and services directly or indirectly associated with fuel. This step will present additional burdens for Sudanese citizens, who are already suffering from low purchasing power.

The government may have dodged the bullet of an Arab Spring that nearly ravaged Sudan, a country already dealing with several separate insurgencies in Darfur (in the west) and in the two border states of Blue Nile and South Kordofan (in the south). Still, the social situation of Sudanese citizens remains harsh and unenviable.

Other Countries Impacted by the Arab Spring

There have been other minor protests, which broke out in Mauritania, Oman, Saudi Arabia, Djibouti, and West Sahara. In Mauritania,[16] the protests were largely peaceful, demanding President Mohamed Ould Abdel Aziz to institute political, economic, and legal reforms. The common themes of these protests included slavery, which officially is illegal in Mauritania but is widespread in the country,[17] and other human rights abuses the opposition has accused the government of perpetrating.

These protests started in January 2011 and continued well into 2012. In Oman[18] demonstrations were demanding salary increases, increased job creation and fighting corruption. The sultan's responses included dismissal of one third of his government cabinet.[19] In Saudi Arabia[20] the protests started with a self-immolation in Samtah and demonstration in the streets of Jeddah in late January 2011. It then was followed by protests against anti-Shia discrimination in February and early March of the same year in Qatif, Hofuf, al-Awamiyah, and Riyadh. In Djibouti[21] the protests, which showed a clear support of the Arab Spring, ended quickly after mass arrests and exclusion of international observers. Lastly, in Western Sahara[22] the protests were a reaction to the failure of police to prevent anti-Sahrawi looting in the city of Dakhla, Western Sahara, and mushroomed into protests across the territory. They were related to the Gdeim Izik protest camp in Western Sahara established the previous fall, which resulted in violence between Sahrawi activists and Moroccan security forces and supporters.

Still, there were still other related events outside of the region. In April 2011,[23] also known among protesters as the Ahvaz *Day of Rage*, protests occurred in Iranian Khuzestan by the Arab minority. These violent protests erupted on April 15, 2011, marking the anniversary of the 2005 Ahvaz unrest. These protests lasted for four days and resulted in about a dozen protesters killed and many more wounded and arrested. Israel also experienced its share of political conflicts with border clashes in May 2011,[24] to commemorate what the Palestinians observe as *Nakba Day*. During the demonstrations, various groups of people attempted to approach or breach Israel's borders from the Palestinian-controlled territory, Lebanon, Syria, Egypt, and Jordan.

Risks related to political instability cannot be eliminated completely, but multinational businesses can take steps to limit the potential effects on their operations. Therefore, before instability develops, businesses should have well-tested business continuity and crisis management plans in place. Organizations should identify their essential functions and assess the potential impact of unrest in various countries, taking into consideration customers, employees, and other key stakeholders.

Assessing Political Risks

As barriers to international trade easel, the dynamic global marketplace continues to attract investors who are eager to capitalize on opportunities they see in emerging markets around the world. Compared to a quarter century ago, these markets enjoy greater stability and are experiencing steady growth. However, these emerging markets remain vulnerable to a host of forces known as political risk that are largely beyond the control of investors. Among these risk factors are currency instability, corruption, weak government institutions, unreformed financial systems, patchy legal and regulatory regimes, and restrictive labor markets.

Multinational corporations and international business professionals can be affected by political risk even when their own operations are in less volatile regions. For instance, supply chains can be impacted, making it critical for businesses to ensure that their suppliers and other partners have robust risk management plans, while simultaneously making alternative suppliers part of resiliency planning.

To help protect personnel, operations, and assets, multinational corporations should consider taking proactive steps by:

- Providing personnel and business partners with regular updates about local government travel advisories.
- Monitoring airlines' flight schedules and status.
- Maintaining up-to-date locations and travel plans for all employees and enabling them to report their status.
- Communicating with staff in affected countries to gain advice or provide information about changes to their situation.

The last bullet, communication, is a very important aspect for proactively dealing with risks at a foreign country. In a crisis, communication is crucial but could be hampered by government interference, damage to communications networks, loss of power, or other factors. In our consulting work, we always advise out clients to consider local conditions before traveling or sending their personnel abroad, including the use of technology (satellite phones, alternative currency, safe house, international insurance and evacuation services, such as International S.O.S,* etc.). Companies and professionals operating in risky international regions should maintain current and complete contact information for employees, including personal e-mail addresses and mobile numbers, so that they can be reached through as many channels as possible. If appropriate, organizations also should consider the use of satellite phones or other technologies that may be more reliable during a crisis.

Corporations also should maintain frequent contact with local embassies, consulates, and other government representatives, which may be able to assist their nationals with communications or evacuations in a crisis. Prior to an event, businesses should have employee citizenship

---

* International SOS is the world's leading medical and travel security services company. They provide assistance to organizations in protecting their people across the globe. Their services are spread across more than 700 locations in 76 countries. For more information check http://www.internationalsos.com/en/

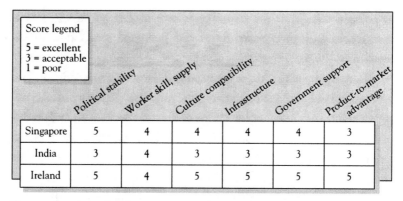

Score legend 5 = excellent 3 = acceptable 1 = poor	Political stability	Worker skill, supply	Culture compatibility	Infrastructure	Government support	Product-to-market advantage
Singapore	5	4	4	4	4	3
India	3	4	3	3	3	3
Ireland	5	4	5	5	5	5

Figure 3.3 Sample of a country profiling assessment matrix

information, including passports, visas, and other travel documents on hand.

Assessment techniques for political risk are as wide-ranging as the sources that generate it. Traditional methods for assessing political risk range from the comparative techniques of rating and mapping systems, as depicted in Figure 3.3, to the analytical techniques of special reports, dynamic segmentation, expert systems, and probability determination to the econometric techniques of model building and discriminant and logit analysis.* These techniques are very useful for identifying and analyzing individual sources of political risk but aren't sophisticated enough to handle cross relationships or correlations well. They also are not accurate measurements of levels of loss generated by the risks being analyzed. Hence, it is difficult to evaluate country profiling and analysis into a practical decision making tool.

In Dr. Goncalves' lectures at Nichols College, when analyzing the inter-dynamics of advanced economies and emerging markets, two approaches are used for incorporating political risk in the capital budgeting process for foreign direct investments. The first approach involves an ad hoc adjustment of the discount rate to account for losses due

---

* Logit analysis is a statistical technique used by marketers to assess the scope of customer acceptance of a product, particularly a new product. It attempts to determine the intensity or magnitude of customers' purchase intentions and translates that into a measure of actual buying behavior.

to political risk, while the second approach involves an ad hoc adjustment of the project's expected future cash flows and expected return on
investment (ROI).

No company, domestic or international, large or small, can conduct
business abroad without considering the influence of the political environment in which it will operate. One of the most undeniable and crucial
realities of international business is that both host and home governments
are integral partners. A government controls and restricts a company's
activities by encouraging and offering support or by discouraging and
restricting its activities contingent upon the whim of the government.

International law recognizes the sovereign right of a nation to grant or
withhold permission to do business at the privileges of the government.
In addition, international law recognizes the sovereign right of a nation to
grant or withhold permission to do business within its political boundaries and to control where its citizens conduct business.

In the context of international law, a sovereign state is independent
and free from all external control; enjoys full legal equality with other
states; governs its own territory; selects its own political, economic, and
social systems; and has the power to enter into agreements with other
nations. Sovereignty refers to both the powers exercised by a state in relation to other countries and the supreme powers exercised over its own
members. A state outlines and decides the requirements for citizenship,
defines geographical boundaries, and controls trade and the movement of
people and goods across its borders.

Nations can and do abridge specific aspects of their sovereign rights in
order to coexist with other nations. The European Union, UN, NAFTA,
NATO, and WTO represent examples of nations voluntarily agreeing
to succumb some of their sovereign rights in order to participate with
member nations for a common, mutually beneficial goal. However, U.S.
involvement in international political affiliations is surprisingly low. For
example, the WTO is considered by some as the biggest threat, thus far
to national sovereignty. Adherence to the WTO inevitably means loss to
some degree of national sovereignty because member nations have pledged
to abide by international covenants and arbitration procedures. Sovereignty was one of the primary issues at the core of a kerfuffle between the
United States and the EU over Europe's refusal to lower tariffs and quotas

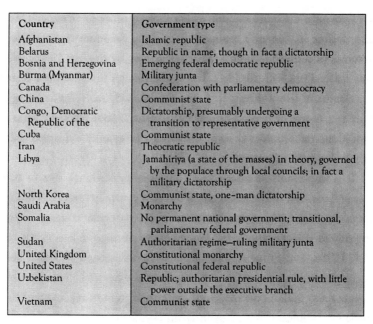

Country	Government type
Afghanistan	Islamic republic
Belarus	Republic in name, though in fact a dictatorship
Bosnia and Herzegovina	Emerging federal democratic republic
Burma (Myanmar)	Military junta
Canada	Confederation with parliamentary democracy
China	Communist state
Congo, Democratic Republic of the	Dictatorship, presumably undergoing a transition to representative government
Cuba	Communist state
Iran	Theocratic republic
Libya	Jamahiriya (a state of the masses) in theory, governed by the populace through local councils; in fact a military dictatorship
North Korea	Communist state, one-man dictatorship
Saudi Arabia	Monarchy
Somalia	No permanent national government; transitional, parliamentary federal government
Sudan	Authoritarian regime—ruling military junta
United Kingdom	Constitutional monarchy
United States	Constitutional federal republic
Uzbekistan	Republic; authoritarian presidential rule, with little power outside the executive branch
Vietnam	Communist state

Figure 3.4 A sampling of government types

on bananas. Critics of the free trade agreements with both South Korea and Peru claim America's sacrifice of sovereignty goes too far.

Figure 3.4 provides a sampling of countries electing other options including authoritarianism, theocracy, dictatorship, and communism, which are taking a different approach. Troubling is the apparent regression of some countries toward autocracy and away from democracy, such as Nigeria, Kenya, Bangladesh, Venezuela, Georgia, and Kyrgyzstan. It is transparent for all to witness the world's greatest experiment in political and economic change: the race between Russian reforms and Chinese gradualism as communism is further left behind in both countries.

Economic and cultural nationalism, which exists to some degree within all countries, is another important risk factor when assessing the international business environment. Nationalism can best be described as an intense feeling of national pride and unity. One of the economic nationalism's central aims is the preservation of economic autonomy whereby residents identify their interests with that preservation of the sovereignty. Hence, national interests and security become far more important than international business relations.

Generally, the more a country feels threatened by some outside force or a decline in domestic economy is evident, the more nationalistic it becomes in protecting itself against intrusions. By the late 1980s, militant nationalism had subsided. Today, the foreign investor, once feared as a dominant tyrant threatening economic development, is often sought after as a source of needed capital investment. Nationalism vacillates as conditions and attitudes change, and foreign companies welcomed today may be harassed tomorrow.

It is important for international business professionals not to confuse nationalism, whose animosity is directed generally toward all foreign countries, with a widespread fear directed at a particular country. Toyota committed this mistake in the United States during the late 1980s and early 1990s. At the time Americans considered the economic threat from Japan greater than the military threat from the Soviet Union. So when Toyota spent millions on an advertising campaign showing Toyotas being made by Americans in a plant in Kentucky, it exacerbated the fear that the Japanese were "colonizing" the United States. The same sentiments ring true with China, who some believe, is colonizing the United States.[25]

The United States is not immune to these same types of directed negativity. The rift between France and the United States over the Iraq/U.S. war led to hard feelings on both sides and an American backlash against French wine, French cheese, and even products Americans thought were French. French's mustard felt compelled to issue a press release stating that it was an American company founded by an American named French. Thus, it is quite clear that no nation-state, however secure, will tolerate penetration by a foreign company into its market and economy if it perceives a social, cultural, economic, or political threat to its well-being.

Various types of political risks should be considered before deciding to expand businesses or invest in foreign markets, for both advanced and emerging economies, but in particularly for frontier markets. The most severe political risk is confiscation, that is, the seizing of a company's assets without payment. The two most notable recent confiscations of U.S. property occurred when Fidel Castro became the leader in Cuba and later when the Shah of Iran was overthrown. Confiscation was most prevalent in the 1950s and 1960s when many underdeveloped countries saw confiscation, albeit ineffective, as a means of economic growth.

risk of type [handwritten margin note]

Less drastic, but still severe, is expropriation, when the government seizes an investment but some reimbursement for the assets is made. Often the expropriated investment is nationalized, that is, it becomes a government-run entity. An example is Bolivia, where the president, Ivo Morales, confiscated Red Eletrica, a utility company from Spain.

A third type of risk is domestication. This occurs when host countries gradually induce the transfer of foreign investments to national control and ownership through a series of government decrees by mandating local ownership and greater national involvement in a company's management. Figure 3.5 provides a sample list of country rankings in terms of political risks when operating a business.

Operational risk

Countries, September 2008 (September 2007 score, if different)

Least risky			Most risky		
Rank		**Score***	**Rank**		**Score**
1	Switzerland	8 (7)	150	Iraq	84 (88)
2	Denmark	10 (8)	149	Guinea	80 (79)
	Singapore	10	148	Myanmar	79 (78)
	Sweden	10	147	Zimbabwe	78 (77)
5	Finland	12 (10)	146	Turkmenistan	77
6	Austria	14		Uzbekistan	77
	Luxembourg	14	144	Venezuela	75 (74)
	Norway	14	143	Tajikistan	71 (70)
9	Netherlands	15 (13)	142	Eritrea	70 (69)
	Britain	15 (12)	141	Chad	68
11	Canada	16 (15)		Ecuador	68
	Hong Kong	16	139	Kenya	66
13	France	17 (16)	138	Côte d'Ivoire	65
	Germany	17 (16)		Nigeria	65 (67)
15	Australia	18 (16)		Sudan	65
	Belgium	18			
	Malta	18 (19)			

* Out of 100, with higher numbers indicating more risk.

Figure 3.5 Country ranking by political and operating risks

Source: The Economist Intelligence Unit

Even though expropriation and confiscation are waning, international companies are still confronted with a variety of economic risks that can occur with little warning. Restraints on business activity may be imposed under the banner of national security to protect an infant industry, to conserve scarce foreign exchange, to raise revenue, or to retaliate against unfair trade practices. Following are important and recurring reality of economic risks, and recurring of the international political environment, that few international companies can avoid:

- **Exchange control:** These stem from shortages of foreign exchange held by a country.
- **Import restrictions:** These are selective restrictions on the import of raw materials, machines, and spare parts; fairly common strategies to force foreign industry to purchase more supplies within the host country and thereby create markets for local industry.
- **Labor problems:** In many countries, labor unions have strong government support that they use effectively in obtaining special concessions from business. Layoffs may be forbidden, profits may have to be shared, and an extraordinary number of services may have to be provided.
- **Local-content laws:** In addition to restricting imports of essential supplies to force local purchase, countries often require a portion of any product sold within the country to have local content, that is, to contain locally made parts.
- **Price controls:** Essential products that command considerable public interest, such as pharmaceuticals, food, gasoline, and cars, are often subjected to price controls. Such controls applied during inflationary periods can be used to control the cost of living. They also may be used to force foreign companies to sell equity to local interests. A side effect could be slowing or even halting capital investment.
- **Tax controls:** Taxes must be classified as a political risk when used as a means of controlling foreign investments. In such cases, they are raised without warning and in violation of formal agreements.

Boycotting is another risk, whereby one or a group of nations might impose it on another, using political sanctions, which effectively stop trade between the countries. The United States has come under criticism for its demand for continued sanctions against Cuba and its threats of future sanctions against countries that violate human rights issues. History, however, indicates that sanctions are almost always unsuccessful in reaching desired goals, particularly when other nations' traders ignore them.

International business professionals traveling to emerging markets or even, to the so called least develop countries (LDCs), must be aware of any travel warnings related to political, health, or terrorism risks. The U.S. Department of State (DOS) provides country specific information for every country. For each country, there is information related to location of the U.S. embassy or consular offices in that country, whether a visa is necessary, crime and security information, health and medical conditions, drug penalties, and localized hot spots. This is an invaluable resource when assessing country risks.

The DOS also issue *travel alerts* for short-term events important for travelers when planning a trip abroad. Issuing a travel alert might include an election season that is bound to have many strikes, demonstrations, disturbances; a health alert like an outbreak of H1N1; or evidence of an elevated risk of terrorist attacks. When these short-term events conclude, the DOS cancels the alert.

During early summer 2014, the DOS issued a Worldwide Caution* to update information on the continuing threat of terrorist actions and violence throughout the world. The report recommended travelers to maintain a high level of vigilance and to take appropriate steps to increase their security awareness, as the Department was concerned about the continued threat of terrorist attacks, demonstrations, and other violent actions. According to the report, kidnappings and hostage events involving U.S. citizens have become increasingly prevalent as al-Qa'ida and its affiliates have increased attempts to finance their operations through kidnapping for ransom operations. Al-Qa'ida in the Arabian Peninsula (AQAP) and al-Qa'ida in the Islamic Maghreb (AQIM) are particularly effective with

---

* http://travel.state.gov/content/passports/english/alertswarnings/worldwide-caution.html

kidnapping for ransom and are using ransom money to fund the range of their activities.

Kidnapping targets are usually Western citizens from governments or third parties that have established a pattern of paying ransoms for the release of individuals in custody. The DOS report also suggested that al-Qa'ida, its affiliated organizations, and other terrorist groups continue to plan and encourage kidnappings of U.S. citizens and Westerners. The Report also suggested that al-Qa'ida and its affiliated organizations continue to plan terrorist attacks against U.S. interests in multiple regions, including Europe, Asia, Africa, and the Middle East. These attacks typically employ a wide variety of tactics including suicide operations, assassinations, kidnappings, hijackings, and bombings. But such extremists can also elect to use conventional or non-conventional weapons, and target both official and private interests. Examples of such targets include high-profile sporting events, residential areas, business offices, hotels, clubs, restaurants, places of worship, schools, public areas, shopping malls, and other tourist destinations both in the United States and abroad where U.S. citizens and Westerns gather in large numbers, including during holidays.

Travel warnings are very important to follow, as the DOS issues them when it wants travelers to consider carefully whether to enter into the country at all. Reasons for issuing a travel warning might include an unstable government, civil war, ongoing intense crime or violence, or frequent terrorist attacks. The U.S. government wants international travelers to know the risks of traveling to these places and to strongly consider not going at all. These travel warnings remain in place until the situation changes. Some have been in effect for years. They are often issued when long-term, protracted conditions lead the State Department to recommend Americans avoid or consider the risk of travel to that country. A *travel warning** also is issued when the U.S. Government's ability to assist American citizens is constrained due to the closure of an embassy

---

* Such information changes often, so we advise you to check the website for up-to-date information at http://travel.state.gov/travel/travel_1744.html, last accessed on 10/10/2013.

Type	Date	Location
① Warning	June 19, 2014	Kenya travel warning
① Warning	June 16, 2014	Iraq travel warning
① Warning	June 12, 2014	Republic of south Sudan travel warning
△ Alert	June 12, 2014	Russian federation travel alert
① Warning	June 8, 2014	Djibouti travel warning
① Warning	June 5, 2014	Ukraine travel warning
① Warning	June 4, 2014	Venezuela travel warning
△ Alert	May 29, 2014	2014 Hurricane and typhoon season
△ Alert	May 28, 2014	Thailand travel alert
① Warning	May 27, 2014	Libya travel warning
① Warning	May 22, 2014	Iran travel warning
① Warning	May 20, 2014	North Korea travel warning
① Warning	May 19, 2014	Philippines travel warning
① Warning	May 13, 2014	Central African republic travel warning
① Warning	May 6, 2014	Nigeria travel warning
① Warning	May 5, 2014	Syria travel warning
① Warning	April 25, 2014	El Salvador travel warning
① Warning	April 25, 2014	Cameroon travel warning
① Warning	April 23, 2014	Democratic republic of the Congo travel warning
① Warning	April 15, 2014	Chad travel warning
① Warning	April 14, 2014	Colombia travel warning

Figure 3.6 List of countries in the U.S. Department of State travel-warning list as of June 2014

Source: U.S. Department of State

or consulate or because of a drawdown of its staff. As of June 2014, the countries listed in Figure 3.6 meet those criteria.

Managing Political Risk

Elisabeth Boone, chartered property casualty underwriter (CPCU) and manager of political risk and credit at ACE Global Markets,[26] argues that very few companies actually have a formal approach to risk management when it comes to emerging markets. She indicates that although the great majority of companies she surveys and advise are aware that political risk management is important to their operations, just 49 percent of them integrate it formally into their investment process, while 41 percent take an informal approach to considering political risk as part of their investment process. This gap between awareness of political risk and formal action to manage it, Boone argues, is serious cause for concern given the fact that 79 percent of her survey respondents reported that their investments in emerging markets had increased over the past three years.

Not surprising, in the post-9/11 era is another survey finding that Boone deems noteworthy. She argues that there is "a perception that terrorism is a greater or at least an equal risk to U.S. assets as political risk, but if you look at the severity of what a confiscation would do to your balance sheet, I believe you'd want to consider political risk as an equal or greater threat in terms of lost investments."*

Indeed, as discussed earlier, in some emerging markets governments seize foreign assets wholesale. In other areas they go after entire sectors. According to Boone, "We're seeing that in mining, oil and gas, and telecommunications. So it's not that they get one of your facilities; they take the whole thing. If you couple that risk with the fact that you don't have an actual risk management process in place, the question becomes: What do you do if you're hit?"†

With emerging markets in every corner of the globe, some challenges for international business professionals and investors are bound to be specific to a particular country or political system. To answer the question of how to manage emerging market risk, you first have to define what is emerging market risk. Essentially, it's volatility and uncertainty. Again, according to Boone, if "you're in a place where there are unstable political, social, and economic conditions, are you able to clearly identify the risks? And if you have identified them, do you have a backup plan for how to respond to a crisis when it happens?"‡ Once you've made that investment you have to continue to monitor and manage the risk.

---

* Ibidem.
† Ididem.
‡ Ididem.

When considering emerging markets you must find ways to manage risks introduced by unstable and less predictable governments. International business professionals and investors may be faced with an uncertain legal environment, environmental and healthcare issues, volatile employment and labor relations, and the involvement of NGOs (non governmental organizations). It is important to consider reputational risk as well; being targeted by companies or countries that go after you for any reason.

For example, hedging corporate assets, insuring its resources (including personnel, equipment, properties, etc.) during the course of a project abroad is very important. Before an event or trip, organizations should develop claim management plans that establish clear roles and responsibilities for personnel inside and outside of the organization. As discussed in this chapter, instability can develop quickly. Hence, it is strongly advisable that key records, including insurance policies, contact lists, and financial and property records, should be accessible in hard copy and electronic formats via local and alternative location sources.

In the event of a loss, organizations should begin to gather data for a claim filing. This includes capturing potential loss information and additional costs associated with the claim, including temporary repairs, extra expenses, and business interruption loss of income costs. Businesses should record photographic and/or video evidence of damage and maintain open lines of communication between employees, insurers, and claims advisors to support policy loss mitigation and notification terms.

There are a few great companies, such as ACE Global Markets,* that cover emerging market risks and focus on three areas: political insurance, trade credit, and trade credit insurance. Political risk insurance covers investments and trade by addressing confiscation of assets as well as interruption of trade in emerging markets due to political events. They also manage structured trade credit, short and medium term, and offer trade credit insurance.

---

* www.aceglobalmarkets.com

CHAPTER 4

FCPA

Dealing With Corruption and Crime

Overview

For the last 20 years, we have witnessed rapid development in the effort to combat corruption under international law, as we now live in a world where, according to Transparency International,[1] and as illustrated in Figure 4.1, more than one in four people report having paid a bribe. International criminals and dishonest businessmen don't hesitate to make use of loose regulatory systems put in place by politicians in certain "safe haven" countries around the world to attract capital.

Currently two regional anti-corruption conventions are in force. The first convention was negotiated and adopted by the members of the Organization of American States (OAS),* while the second was adopted under the auspices of the Organization for Economic Co-operation and Development (OECD)[†]. In addition, a number of international organizations are vigorously working on developing appropriate anti-corruption measures. These groups include several bodies within the UN, the EU, and the International Bank for Reconstruction and Development (IBRD), also known as the World Bank Group (WB). Also involved are

---

* Organization of American States: Inter-American Convention Against Corruption, Mar. 29, 1996, 35 I.L.M. 724.

[†] Convention on Combating Bribery of Foreign Public Officials in International Business Transactions, Done at Paris, Dec. 18, 1997, 37 I.L.M. The OECD Convention was signed on November 21, 1997, by the twenty-six member countries of the Organization of Economic Co-operation and Development and by five nonmember countries: Argentina, Brazil, Bulgaria, Chile and the Slovak Republic.

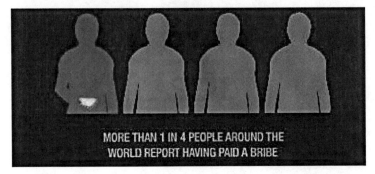

Figure 4.1 More than one in four people around the world report having paid a bribe

Source: Transparency International

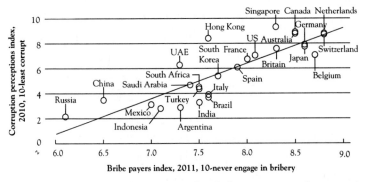

Figure 4.2 The perceived corruption levels by country and companies' propensity to bribe

Source: Transparency International

several nongovernmental organizations, such as Transparency International and the International Chamber of Commerce (ICC).

Figure 4.2 provides the perceived corruption levels by country and companies' propensity for bribery. The higher the score means fewer propensities to bribe.

When journalists with the Center for Investigative Journalism in Bucharest, Romania started investigating a gold mining operation in the village of Rosia Montana, in the heart of Transylvania, they didn't know they would soon be looking at a far wider web of corruption that linked commercial enterprises on five continents. The name of a company and the name of its founder led the journalists to Russian oligarchs, officials in Eastern European governments, former employees of well-known corporations and even NATO* officials.

The tangled network of connections unraveled as journalists looked deeper and deeper at corporate records in over 20 countries. Company records exposed the connections between former Communist government officials and devious, Western-based companies. They also revealed that big chunks of Eastern European economies still are handled by former employees of the Communist Secret Services.

In another example, a name on a corporate record in Bulgaria led to an investigation involving the Irish Republican Army's (IRA) money laundering through purchases of real estate on the shores of the Black Sea. A company record in Hungary led to one of the most powerful Russian organized crime bosses and his questionable interests in the natural gas industry.

When we consider these examples, and there are numerous news outlets around the world show casing many more, we also must consider ways of responding to the challenges of dealing with international corruption and crime, not only as international business investors and professionals, but also as a responsible global society. Corruption not only disrupts businesses, but also generates social imbalances and poverty. The international response to corruption, therefore, raises many important questions:

- Could global corruption and crime be a manifestation of oppression around the world?
- Is the anti-corruption movement a global outcry against the abuse of power?
- Is the pressure on trade competition around the globe promoting corruption?
- Is global corruption a result of globalization?
- Is the anti-corruption movement a consequence of a renewed sense of morality around the world?
- Should global corruption be a concern for international law?

---

* NATO is an international organization composed of the U.S., Canada, UK, and a number of European countries, established by the North Atlantic Treaty (1949) for purposes of collective security.

While certainly provoked by these questions, this chapter does not pretend to give definitive answers. It seeks only to contribute to the understanding of the development of anti-corruption measures under the international law, since, according to the United Nations Interregional Crime and Justice Research Institute (UNICRI), corruption today is one of the main threats to global development and security.* Corruption and crime often is considered the negative side of globalization as international crime has been rapidly capitalizing on the expansion of global trade and broadening its range of activities. Several criminal groups, organized as multinational companies, are often seeking profits through the evaluation of countries' risks, benefits, and markets analysis.

Challenges of Fighting Global Corruption

Corruption around the world is facilitated by the ability to launder and hide proceeds derived from the abuse of power, bribery, and secret deals. Dirty money enters the financial system and is given the semblance of originating from a legitimate source, often by using corporate vehicles offering disguise, concealment, and anonymity. For instance, corrupt politicians used secret companies to obscure their identity in 70 percent of more than 200 cases of grand corruption surveyed by the World Bank.

The Economist ran a piece, back in 2011, about "harassment bribes," or the small bribes citizens in India must pay in order to receive routine public services. Under the current system, someone who makes this kind of payment is equally liable under the law as the person who accepts the bribe. The proposed law change would allow citizens to file complaints, free from fear of prosecution, and also to receive a refund for their coerced payments. The payer of a harassment bribe would no longer face legal penalties, hence the legalization of the bribe-giving. The receiver of the bribe, however, would still be engaging in illegal activity. It is an untested and provocative idea that tries to weaken the demand side of corruption and repay its victims. The approach demonstrates how old problems can be addressed from a new perspective.

---

* http://www.unicri.it/topics/organized_crime_corruption/

For far too long, crooked figures have been able to stash the proceeds of corruption easily in foreign banks or to invest them in luxurious mansions, expensive cars, or lavish lifestyles. They do this with impunity and in blatant disregard for the citizens or customers they are supposed to serve.

Most importantly, there are several complacent and sometimes complicit governments of countries with banking centers that facilitate money laundering and allow the corrupt to cross their borders to enjoy stolen wealth. Weak government actions are failing to prevent the corrupt from evading justice and have enabled cross-border transfers of corrupt assets. Complacent governments responsible for protecting the public from such criminal acts are de facto supporting impunity for corruption.

For entities fighting crime and corruption around the world, one of the main challenges, therefore, consists of preventing such groups from continuously adapting to the changes at local and international levels. It is important to disrupt the creation of intercontinental networks, and prevent them from diversifying their activities and taking advantage of the potential offered by globalization. These factors are the main obstacles for all entities around the world fighting organized crime. Furthermore, the lack of judicial and enforcement tools plays a strategic role in the growth of global criminal syndicates' management of trafficking drugs, arms, human beings, counterfeiting, and money laundering.

Under the veil of banking and commercial secrecy laws, huge amounts of money exchange hands in havens outside jurisdiction scrutiny of the source countries. Capital cycled through such dealings can be transformed into real estate, bonds, or other goods and then moved back into the country or to other global markets legitimately. Such transactions are closely looked at by international law enforcement because they raise suspicion of money laundering associated with organized crime and terrorism.

Although off-shore havens usually are associated with tropical islands somewhere in the Caribbean, in many instances countries such as Austria, Switzerland, or the United States have off-shore-like facilities that enable businesses and individuals to hide ownership and deter investigators from finding out who owns companies that are involved in crooked deals.

Organized crime figures would rather use *private foundations* (Privat-stiftungs) in Austria, or companies in the state of Delaware in the United States, than companies in the British Virgin Islands (BVI), the Isle of Man, Aruba, or Liberia, known as safe havens that the media and law enforcement have associated as a places for money laundering. The mere mention of any of these places can mark a red flag on a transaction that then is monitored by international law enforcement.

All over the world, organized crime adopts all forms of corruption to infiltrate political, economic, and social levels. Although strong institutions, in particular government ones, are supposed to be impermeable to corruption, weak governance often coexists with corruption and a mutually causal connection exists between corruption and feeble governmental institutions, which often ends up in a vicious cycle. Hence, well-known offshore havens are fighting to clean up their names and show that proper control mechanisms are in place. It should be mentioned that in most cases, such jurisdictions are now used for tax purposes.

For instance, Liechtenstein, a European country of 35,000 people located in the Alps, was hit hard in the beginning of 2008 when data stolen by a former bank employee was sold to law enforcement agencies in many European countries. The data showed that wealthy citizens from many countries had used Liechtenstein's banks in tax evasion schemes. As a result of the leak, the German authorities who bought the disks managed to recover over $150 million in back taxes within months of obtaining the data. The United States, Canada, Australia, and the EU countries are also in possession of the same data and they are independently pursuing their own investigations into tax evasions involving banking in the tiny country.

The scandal not only shook Liechtenstein's political relationships with other countries but spread to Switzerland and Luxembourg, two other European countries that have a record of bank secrecy and nontransparent financial transactions. The head of the Swiss Bankers' Association, Pierre Mirabaud, was so outraged by the fact that the stolen data ended up in German law enforcement's hands that he said in an interview with a Swiss TV station that the methods German investigators' methods reminded him of Gestapo practices, referring to the secret police of Nazi-era Germany. He later apologized for the unfortunate comparison. Just like Liechtenstein, Cyprus has been blamed many times for harboring money from organized crime groups and former communist officials from Eastern European countries.

The growing problem of offshore havens, corruption, and crime, and the damage they bring to the global economy, has been pointed out repeatedly in the context of the global financial crisis. The OECD together with French and German government leaders vowed to make the offshore industry *disappear*. They called the offshore areas the *black holes of global finance*.[2] The offshore company formation industry, however, is kept alive by scores of lawyers, incorporation agents and solicitors. They advertise complex business schemes to maximize returns and minimize taxation.

Take for example the website http://www.off-shore.co.uk/faq/company-formation/ which explicitly presents potential customers with the possibility of hiding real ownership of a company behind a nominee shareholder or director. According to the site's frequently asked questions (FAQ) section,

> A nominee shareholder or director is a third party who allows his/her name to be used in place of the real or beneficial owner and director of the company. The nominee is advised particularly in those jurisdictions where the names of the officers are part of a public record, open for anyone who cares to look can find out these identities. The name of the nominee will appear and ensure the privacy of the beneficial owner.

The primary role of such company formation schemes is to avoid paying taxes. However, some countries go to extremes when they try to hide the real beneficial owners. Panama and Liberia are among the countries that go to great lengths to preserve the anonymity of company owners. Under Panamanian law, an *S.A. corporation** can be owned by the physical holder of certificates or shares, with no recorded owner in any database or public registry. In fact, there is no public registry in Panama, so the government does not even know who owns shares in corporations. Shares

---

* Designates a type of corporation in countries that mostly employ civil law. Depending on language, it means anonymous society, anonymous company, anonymous partnership, or Share Company, roughly equivalent to public limited company in common law jurisdictions.

can exchange hands at any time and the beneficial owners are impossible to trace through public records.

Discerning the ownership of companies trading around the world has become increasingly complex. A company in Belgrade, Serbia, could be owned by a firm in Rotterdam, the Netherlands, which could in turn be owned by a private foundation in Austria that has Russian oligarchs as its beneficial owners. This is a common scheme. Investigative journalists in the Balkans have identified schemes as complicated as twenty layers of companies. Searches performed for names of such companies often lead to lawyers or designated shareholders. But this should not be seen as a dead or a fait accompli. Organized crime figures quite often rely on the same lawyers or the same formation agent when they establish new companies to limit the number of people aware of their moves. Once a lawyer or straw party is identified, searches of the lawyer's name can be performed on various databases. This could reveal dozens or hundreds of companies associated with the solicitor's name.

Therefore, as mentioned earlier in this chapter, corruption is a challenge not only for emerging markets but also for advanced economies. In the United States, as a result of the U.S. Securities and Exchange Commission (SEC) investigations in the mid-1970s, over 400 U.S. companies admitted making questionable or illegal payments in excess of $300 million dollars to foreign government officials, politicians, and political parties. The abuses ran the gamut from bribery of high foreign officials to securing some type of favorable action by a foreign government to so-called facilitating payments that were made to ensure that government functionaries discharged certain ministerial or clerical duties.

One major example is the aerospace company Lockheed bribery scandals, in which its officials paid foreign officials to favor their company's products.[3] Another example is the *Bananagate* scandal in which Chiquita™ Brands bribed the president of Honduras to lower taxes.*

Congress enacted the Foreign Corrupt Practices Act (FCPA), which is discussed in more detail later in this chapter, to bring a halt to the bribery of foreign officials and to restore public confidence in the integrity

---

* "Banana tax raised." Facts on File World News Digest. May 3 1975.

of the American business system. The Act was signed into law by President Jimmy Carter on December 19, 1977, and amended in 1998 by the International Anti-Bribery Act of 1998 that was designed to implement the anti-bribery conventions of the OECD. The FCPA makes it a crime for any American citizen and business to bribe foreign public officials for business purposes. It also imposes certain accounting standards on public U.S. companies.

Corruption Generates Poverty

Being poor not only means falling below a certain income line. Poverty is a multi-dimensional phenomenon that is often characterized by a series of different factors, including access to essential services (health, education, sanitation, and so on), basic civil rights, empowerment, and human development.[4] Corruption undermines these development pillars, an individual's human rights and the legal frameworks intended to protect them. In countries where governments can pass policies and budgets without consultation or accountability for their actions, undue influence, unequal development and poverty result.[5] People become disempowered (politically, economically, and socially) and, in the process, further impoverished.

In a corrupt environment, wealth is captured, income inequality is increased, and a state's governing capacity is reduced, particularly when it comes to attending to the needs of the poor. For citizens, these outcomes create a scenario that leaves the poor trapped and development stalled, often forcing the poor to rely on bribes and other illegal payments in order to access basic services. Multiple and destructive forces take roots in corrupt country: increased corruption, reduced sustainable growth, and slower rates of poverty reduction.* As warned by the World Bank,

---

* For more information on this theme, see Paolo Mauro, "Corruption and Growth," *Quarterly Journal of Economics*, 110, 681–712 (1995); Sanjeev Gupta, Hamid Davoodi and Rosa Alonso Terme, "Does Corruption Affect Income Equality and Poverty?" IMF Working Paper 98/76 (Washington, DC: IMF, 1998); Paolo Mauro, "The Effects of Corruption on Growth and Public Expenditure," Chapter 20 in Arnold J. Heidenheimer and Michael Johnston (eds.), *Political Corruption: Concepts and Contexts*. 3rd ed. (New Brunswick, NJ: Transaction Publishers, 2002).

corruption is "the greatest obstacle to reducing poverty."* This growing socio-economic inequality causes the loss of confidence in public institutions. Social instability and violence increase because of growing inequality, poverty, and abject mistrust of political leaders and institutions.

When it comes to income inequality, even Alan Greenspan is worried about this troubling trend. As argued by Chrystia Freeland, a Canadian international finance reporter at Thompson Reuters, in her book *Plutocrats*,[6] there has always been a gap between rich and poor in every country around the globe, but recently what it means to be rich has changed dramatically. Forget the one percent as is commonly believed; Plutocrats prove that it is the wealthiest 0.1 percent who are outpacing the rest of us at breakneck speed. Most of these new fortunes are not inherited; they are amassed by perceptive businesspeople that see themselves as deserving victors in a cutthroat competitive world. In her book, Freeland exposes the consequences of concentrating the world's wealth into fewer and fewer hands.

The question Freeland raises is whether the gap between the superrich and the rest is the product of impersonal market forces or political machinations. She draws parallels between current inequality and the Gilded Age of the late 1800s, when the top 1 percent of the U.S. population held one-third of the national income. Globalization and the technological revolutions are the major factors behind what she sees as new and overlapping Gilded Ages: the second for the United States, the first for emerging markets. Drawing on interviews with economists and the elite themselves, Freeland chronicles hand wringing over the direction of the global economy by these 0.1 percent plutocrats around the world. As she laments, the feedback loop between money, politics, and ideas is both cause and consequence of the rise of the super-elite.

Corruption, therefore, often accompanies centralization of power, when leaders are not accountable to those they serve. More directly, corruption inhibits development when leaders help themselves to money that otherwise would be used for development projects. Corruption, both in government and business, places a heavy cost on society. Businesses

---

* www.worldbank.org/anticorruption. Last accessed on 10/10/2012.

should enact, publicize, and follow codes of conduct banning corruption on the part of their staff and directors. Citizens must demand greater transparency on the part of both government and the corporate sector and create reform movements where needed.

Corruption on the part of governments, the private sector ,and citizens affect development initiatives at their core root by skewing decision-making, budgeting and implementation processes. When these actors abuse their entrusted power for private gain, corruption denies the participation of citizens and diverts public resources into private hands. The poor find themselves at the losing end of this corruption chain— without state support and the services they demand. The issue of corruption is also very much inter-related with other issues. On a global level, the economic system that has shaped the current form of globalization in the past decades requires further scrutiny for it also has created conditions whereby corruption can flourish and exacerbate the conditions of people around the world who already have little say about their own destiny.

Corruption is both a major cause and a result of poverty around the world. It occurs at all levels of society, from local and national governments, civil society, judiciary functions, large and small businesses, military and other services, and so on. Corruption, nonetheless, affects the poorest the most, whether in rich or poor nations.

It is difficult to measure or compare, however, the impact of corruption on poverty against the effects of inequalities that are structured into law, such as unequal trade agreements, structural adjustment policies, "free" trade agreements, and so on. The reality is that corruption and crime generate a lot of poverty around the world, especially among the least developed countries (LDC). A list of the top 50 is depicted in Figure 4.3.

To identify corruption is not difficult, but it is harder to see the layers it can have, especially under the more formal, even legal forms of corruption. It is easy to assume that these formal forms are not even an issue because they are often part of the laws and institutions that govern national and international communities of which many of us are accustomed to. If a president of an emerging country gets paid a bribe and as a result taxes are reduced to benefit certain corporations or even markets, what do we, the general public, know?

Figure 4.3 The 50 least developed countries in the world

Source: UNCTAD

Corruption promotes, and often determines, the misuse of governments' resources by diverting them from sectors of vital importance such as health, education, and development. Hence, the people who have the most needs, the poor people, are the ones deprived of economic growth and development opportunities, which in turn causes significant income inequalities and lack of social mobility. Corruption also siphons off goods and money intended to alleviate poverty. These leakages compromise a country's economic growth, investment levels, poverty reduction efforts, and other development-related advances.

At the same time, petty corruption saps the resources of poor people by forcing them to offer bribes in exchange for access to basic goods and services, many of which may be free by law, such as healthcare and education. With few other choices, poor people may resort to corruption as a survival strategy to overcome the exclusion faced when trying to go to school, get a job, buy a house, vote or simply participate in their societies. Consequently, the cost of public services rises to the point where economically deprived people can no longer afford them. As the poor become poorer, corruption feeds poverty and inequality.

Combating poverty and corruption, therefore, means addressing and overcoming the barriers that stand in the way of citizen engagement and a state's accountability. While most emerging economies claim that the equal participation and rights of citizens exist, in reality they rarely apply to the poor. Hence, to be effective, pro-poor anti-corruption strategies must look more closely at the larger context that limits opportunities for poor citizens to participate in political, economic, and social processes.

The Importance of Political Participation and Accountability

Corruption in the political sphere attracts growing attention in more and more countries. The demand for accountability of political leaders and the transparency of political parties has begun to trigger reform in those areas. Private businesses also have become a focus of anti-corruption reform. Besides being the object of state oversight, this sector has started its own initiatives to curb corruption.

Linking the rights of marginalized communities and individuals to seek government's accountability is a fundamental first step for developing a pro-poor anti-corruption strategy. Citizens giving their governments the power to act on their behalf shape a country's policies. Corruption by public and private sector officials taints this process, distorts constitutions and institutions, and results in poverty and unequal development. Strengthening political accountability would result in policies that ensure that the poor are seen not as victims but rather as stakeholders in the fight against corruption. For now, a consensus on how to strengthen these elements into action remains elusive within development cooperation circles.[7]

Notwithstanding the large differences in the problems prevalent in various countries and the existing remedies, it is satisfying to see efforts to prevent corruption target similar areas across the region. Most countries that have endorsed the OECD's Anti-Corruption Action Plan, for example, attribute an important role to administrative reforms. Hence, the various strategies to prevent corruption address integrity, effective procedures, and transparent rules.

The integrity and competence of public officials are fundamental pre-requisites for a reliable and efficient public administration. Many countries in the OECD region have subsequently adopted measures that aim to ensure integrity in the hiring and promoting of staff, provide adequate remuneration, and set and implement clear rules of conduct.

Past and current efforts to reduce poverty suggests that corruption has been a constant obstacle for countries, particularly emerging economies, trying to bring about the political, economic and social changes desired for their development. Across different country contexts, corruption has been a cause and consequence of poverty. At the same time, as depicted in Figure 4.4, corruption is a by-product of poverty. The poorest countries in the world, already marginalized, tend to suffer a double level of exclusion in countries where corruption characterizes the rules of the game. Interestingly enough, oil-producing countries also make the list.

Rank	Country	Score
175	Somalia	8
175	North Korea	8
175	Afghanistan	8
174	Sudan	11
173	South Sudan	14
172	Libya	15
171	Iraq	16
168	Turkmenistan	17
168	Syria	17
168	Uzbekistan	17
167	Yemen	18
163	Equatorial Guinea	19
163	Chad	19
163	Haiti	19
163	Guinea Bissau	19
160	Cambodia	20
160	Eritrea	20
160	Venezuela	20

Figure 4.4 The most corrupt countries in the world

Source: Business Insider

The Foreign Corrupt Practice Act

The FCPA of 1977 is a U.S. federal law known primarily for two of its main provisions. One addresses accounting transparency requirements under the Securities Exchange Act of 1934, and the other concerning bribery of foreign officials.* It was enacted in the surge of public morality following the Watergate Scandal and in response to a U.S. congressional investigation uncovering widespread bribery among domestic companies operating overseas.

The FCPA applies to any person who has a certain degree of connection to the U.S. and engages in foreign corrupt practices. As argued by Alexandro Posadas,[8] of Duke University, the Act governs not only payments to foreign officials, candidates, and parties, but also any other recipient if part of the bribe is ultimately attributable to a foreign official, candidate, or party. These payments are not restricted to monetary forms and may include anything of value.

The meaning of foreign official, however, is broad. For example, an owner of a bank who is also the minister of finance is considered a foreign official according to the U.S. government. Doctors at government-owned or managed hospitals are also considered to be foreign officials under the FCPA, as is anyone working for a government-owned or managed institution or enterprise. Employees of international organizations such as the United Nations are also considered to be foreign officials under the FCPA.

Individuals subject to the FCPA include any U.S. or foreign corporation that has a class of securities registered (public trade companies), or that is required to file reports under the Securities and Exchange (SEC) Act of 1934. The SEC actually has increased the level of FCPA action, as shown in Figure 4.5, from 17 cases in 2007 to 20 cases in 2011.

The U.S. Department of Justice (DOJ), as depicted in Figure 4.6, has ramped up enforcement of the FCPA against individuals. In 2005, less than five individuals were prosecuted, but by 2010 more than 22 individuals were charged with violation. As an example, the former U.S.

---

* US Department of Justice page on the FCPA, including a layperson's guide. Download a free copy of it at http://www.justice.gov/criminal/fraud/fcpa/guide.pdf.

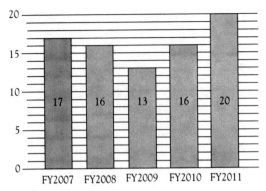

Figure 4.5 FCPA actions brought by the SEC

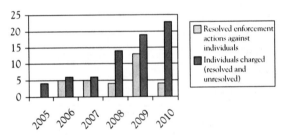

Figure 4.6 Increase in DOJ enforcement of FCPA against individuals

representative William J. Jefferson, democrat of Louisiana, was charged with violating the FCPA for bribing African governments for business interests.[9]

The FCPA also requires companies whose securities are listed in the United States to meet its accounting provisions.* These accounting provisions, which were designed to operate in tandem with the anti-bribery provisions of the FCPA, require corporations covered by the provisions to maintain records that accurately and fairly reflect the transactions of the corporation and to devise and maintain an adequate system of internal accounting controls. An increasing number of corporations are taking additional steps to protect their reputation and reduce exposure by employing the services of due diligence companies. Identifying government-owned companies in an effort to identify easily overlooked

---

* See FCPA Act See 15 U.S.C. § 78m.

government officials is rapidly becoming a critical component of more advanced anti-corruption programs.

Regarding payments to foreign officials, the act draws a distinction between bribery and facilitation or *grease payments*, which may be permissible under the FCPA but may still violate local laws. The primary distinction is that grease payments are made to an official to expedite his performance of the duties he is already bound to perform. Payments to foreign officials may be legal under the FCPA if the payments are permitted under the written laws of the host country. Certain payments or reimbursements relating to product promotion also may be permitted under the FCPA.

FCPA Violations

Recent changes to the United States FCPA now allow individuals to potentially collect millions of dollars by reporting corruption in U.S. companies or any company traded on U.S. exchanges. If a person knows of any improper payments, offers, or gifts made by a company to obtain an advantage in a business in the United States or abroad they are encouraged to report it. There are several law firms in the United States set up to assist whistleblowers in reporting their suspicions. There is no materiality to this act, making it illegal to offer anything of value as a bribe, including cash or noncash items. The government focuses on the intent of the bribery rather than on the amount.

Becoming a FCPA whistleblower may entitle the individual to receive substantial compensation, potentially millions of dollars. New changes in U.S. laws now allow individuals reporting FCPA violations to receive full protection from retaliation and collect up to 30 percent of the fines that the government collects. The U.S. government can fine companies up to $2 million dollars for each violation of the law. Thus for each payment made and each false record there may be a fine levied even if the payments are nominal. In 2010, the U.S. government collected over $1.5 billion in FCPA fines.

In addition, the Travel Act, enacted into law in 1961, forbids the use of travel and communications means to commit state or federal crimes. Ostensibly, it has been used to prosecute domestic crimes, such as the

S. no	Penalty (in $ mil.)	Company	Company's headquarters	Year penalty was assessed
	Eight of the 10 largest settlements for violations of the Foreign Corrupt Practices Act occurred in 2010			
1	$800	Siemens	Germany	2008
2	$579	KBR/Halliburtort	United States	2009
3	$400	BAE Systems	United Kingdom	2010
4	$365	ENI S.p.A/Snamprogetti Netherlands B.V.	Italy/Holland	2010
5	$338	Technip S.A.	France	2010
6	$185	Daimler AG	Germany	2010
7	$137	Alcatel-Lucent	France	2010
8	$82	Panalpina	Switzerland	2010
9	$58	ABB Ltd.	Switzerland	2010
10	$56	Pride International	United States	2010

Figure 4.7 FCPA enforcement: billion-dollar fines and jail time

Source: Hogan Lovells

Racketeer Influenced and Corrupt Organizations Act* (RICO) and gambling violations committed either by individuals or groups of persons.

As depicted in Figure 4.7, some notable examples of FCPA violations include but are not limited to multinational corporations such as Walmart, BAE Systems, Baker Hughes, Daimler AG, Halliburton, KBR, Lucent Technologies, Monsanto, Siemens, Titan™ Corporation, Triton Energy Limited, Avon Products, and Invision Technologies.

In April of 2012 an article in The New York Times reported that a former executive of Walmart de Mexico alleged in September 2005 that Walmart's Mexican subsidiary had paid bribes to officials throughout Mexico in order to obtain construction permits. Investigators of Walmart

---

* Commonly referred to as the RICO Act, this is a U.S. federal law that provides for extended criminal penalties and a civil cause of action for acts performed as part of an ongoing criminal organization. The RICO Act focuses specifically on racketeering, and it allows the leaders of a syndicate to be tried for the crimes which they ordered others to do or assisted them, closing a perceived loophole that allowed someone who told a man to, for example, murder, to be exempt from the trial because he did not actually commit the crime personally.

actually found credible evidence that Mexican and American laws had been broken, which prompted Walmart executives in the United States to *hushed-up* the allegations.[10]

Another article in Bloomberg argued Wal-Mart's "probe of possible bribery in Mexico may prompt executive departures and steep U.S. government fines if it reveals senior managers knew about the payments and didn't take strong enough action, corporate governance experts said."[11] Eduardo Bohorquez, the director of Transparencia Mexicana, a "watchdog" group in Mexico, urged the Mexican government to investigate the allegations.[12] Wal-Mart and the U.S. Chamber of Commerce had participated in a campaign to amend FCPA, where, according to proponents, the changes would clarify the law, while according to opponents, the changes would weaken the law.[13]

In 2008, Siemens AG paid a $450 million fine for violating the FCPA. This was one of the largest penalties ever collected by the DOJ for an FCPA case.* The U.S. Justice Department and the SEC currently are investigating whether Hewlett Packard Company executives paid $10.9 million in bribery money between 2004 and 2006 to the Prosecutor General of Russia "to win a €35 million euros ($47.86 million dollars) contract to supply computer equipment throughout Russia."[14]

In July 2011, the DOJ opened an inquiry into the News International phone hacking scandal that brought down News of the World, the recently closed UK tabloid newspaper. In cooperation with the Serious Fraud Office in the UK, the DOJ is examining whether News Corporation violated the FCPA by bribing British police officers.[15]

In 2012, Japanese firm Marubeni Corporation paid a criminal penalty of $54.6 million for FCPA violations when acting as an agent of the TKSJ joint venture, which comprised of Technip S.A., Snamprogetti Netherlands B.V., Kellogg Brown & Root Inc. (KBR), and JGC Corporation. Between 1995 and 2004, the joint venture won four contracts in Nigeria worth more than $6 billion as a direct result of having paid $51 million to Marubeni for the purpose of bribing Nigerian government officials.[16]

---

* http://www.foreign-corrupt-practices-act.org/foreign-corrupt-practices-act-news/5-siemens-ag-pays-450-million-to-settle-fcpa-bribery-charges.html, (last accessed 08/12/2013).

In March 2012, Biomet Inc. a Warsaw, Indiana company paid a criminal fine of $17.3 million in its settlement with the DOJ, and $5.5 million in disgorgement of profits and pre-judgment interest to the SEC.[17] Biomet had bribed doctors at government hospitals in Argentina, Brazil, and China from 2000 to 2008. It paid out more than $1.5 million and disguised the payments as commissions, royalties, consulting fees, and scientific incentives.

Johnson & Johnson also paid $70 million in 2011 to settle criminal and civil FCPA charges for bribes to public sector doctors in Greece. Its subsidiary DePuy Inc. was charged in a criminal complaint with conspiracy and violations of the FCPA. A former DePuy executive in the UK, Robert John Dougall, was jailed for a year after he pleaded guilty in a London court to making £4.5 million pounds ($7.36 million) in corrupt payments to Greek medical professionals.*

Other settlements for FCPA violations in 2012 include Smith & Nephew,[18] who paid $22.2 million to the DOJ and SEC, and BizJet International Sales and Support Inc.,[19] who paid $11.8 million to the DOJ for bribery of foreign government officials. Both companies entered into a deferred prosecution agreement.

FCPA Criticism

While the FCPA has the unquestionably noble goal of eliminating corruption and holding U.S. concerns to a high standard of morality, it has come under recent criticism for the substantial and, some would say, anti-competitive, costs that it imposes. In December 2011, the New York City Bar Association's Committee on International Business Transactions issued a report critical of the FCPA, and, perhaps more significantly, its enforcement.[20]

The report noted that the FCPA imposes substantial compliance costs on companies subject to its jurisdiction—costs that their foreign competitors may not face. It also lamented the seemingly unchecked prosecutorial power to obtain huge settlements in FCPA cases, as the consequences

---

* Ibidem.

of an FCPA indictment are potentially fatal to a company, and, as a result, most companies are willing to settle for large sums—regardless of whether they believe the allegations are valid. Indeed, as the report notes, in April 2011, each of the eight top fines for FCPA "violations" exceeded $100 million.

The report expressed concern that the U.S. DOJ is both prosecutor and judge in the FCPA context and that some U.S. companies have ceased foreign operations in the face of FCPA uncertainty. To that end, the report makes a number of recommendations to reign in the FCPA, such as adding a "willfulness" requirement before imposing liability on corporations, which can be criminally liable without having knowledge of the wrongful conduct, to ensure that only those companies that intend to violate the law are subject to the harsh fines, as well as a provision limiting a company's successor liability for the premerger FCPA violations of a company that it acquired.

In an article titled *State Hypocrisy on Anti-Bribery Laws*, Stephan Kinsella* argues that the duplicity of

> FCPA is blinding, as it makes it okay for the state to bribe (and extort and coerce) private business by means of threats, subsidies, tax breaks, and protectionist legislation, and okay for businesses to bribe elected officials (campaign contributions), and okay for the U.S. administration to bribe foreign governments, and okay for U.S. companies to be forced to pay bribes in the form of taxes, that are less than the amount of bribes they would have to pay to foreign officials, but not okay for U.S. companies to bribe foreign officials—even if this is customary and essential to "doing business" in that country, despite the fact this puts American businesses at a competitive disadvantage with companies from other countries that do not prohibit such bribery.

---

* Kinsella is an American intellectual property lawyer and libertarian legal theorist. His legal works have been published by Oceana Publications, which was acquired in 2005 by Oxford University Press and West/Thomson Reuters.

As Lew Rockwell,* former congressional chief of staff to U.S. senator Ron Paul, noted in his article *Extortion, Private and Public: The Case of Chiquita Banana,*[†]

> Paying bribes and being subject to this kind of extortion is just part of what it takes to do business in many countries. This might sound awful, but the truth is that such payments are often less than the companies would be paying to the tax man in the U.S., which runs a similar kind of extortion scam but with legal cover.[‡]

In Rockwell's opinion, American businesses are howling at the competitive disadvantage this Act imposes on them. Instead of repealing the FCPA Act, Rockwell argues the United States is using its legislative imperialism to force other countries to adopt similar laws, while twisting the arms of other countries in a number of areas, including intellectual property, antitrust law, central banking policies, oil & gas ownership by the state, environmental standards, labor standards, tax levels and policy, and so on. It did this mainly by pushing the OECD Anti-Bribery Convention, now ratified by 38 states, which are required by the Convention to implement FCPA style laws nationally. The UK has confirmed by creating the UK Bribery Act.[§]

It is important to note that the FCPA does not contain a private right of action. Hence, only the government can enforce the Act. But, private complainants have steadily found creative ways to use FCPA violations as predicated acts in private causes of action. These private actions are often opportunistic in that they usually commence after a

---

* Mr. Rockwell was also the former editorial assistant to Ludwig von Mises institute. He is the founder and chairman of the Mises Institute, and the executor for the estate of Murray N. Rothbard, and editor of LewRockwell.com.
[†] http://archive.lewrockwell.com/rockwell/case-of-chiquita-banana185.html, (last accessed on 12/14/2013).
[‡] Ibidem.
[§] http://www.legislation.gov.uk/ukpga/2010/23/contents.

government investigation has become public, and they use admissions and settlements in the government context to further their own cause of action.

For example, in 2010, Innospec Inc. pleaded guilty to violating the FCPA by bribing officials in Iraq and Indonesia to ensure sales of its product in those areas. It agreed to pay $14.1 million dollars in penalties and to retain an independent compliance monitor for three years to oversee the imposition of an anti-corruption compliance protocol. On the same day, it also settled a civil complaint with the U.S. SEC, requiring it to disgorge $11.2 million dollars in profits.[21]

After Innospec pleaded guilty, its competitor, NewMarket Corp., brought claims against it for antitrust violations.[22] NewMarket claimed that Innospec paid bribes to the Iraqi and Indonesian governments so that those governments would favor Innospec's product, would not transition to NewMarket's product, and would therefore maintain Innospec's monopoly in those markets. Pointedly, NewMarket's principal financial officer, David Fiorenza, said that it was only after reading about the plea that he learned about Innospec's actions,[23] which would eventually form the basis of NewMarket's complaint. This case ultimately settled in October 2011 when Innospec agreed to pay NewMarket $45 million dollars.[24]

The lack of a compliance defense, as shown in Innospec's case, is particularly problematic in the successor liability context, as a company does not have any defense under the FCPA for the corrupt actions of an acquired company, even if the acquiring company adhered to its compliance program by conducting a rigorous due diligence investigation, but ultimately failing to uncover corrupt acts.

In light of government's resistance to amend the FCPA and the pace of recent FCPA enforcement, the addition of a corporate willfulness requirement or a compliance program defense is unlikely in the short term. Nor can one expect to see the elimination of successor liability. With this legal environment, companies should focus on effectively implementing a compliance program, while actively looking for opportunities to ensure that other companies (particularly competitors) are not able to reap the benefits of illegal acts.

Preventing Corruption and Crime through Software and Web-Based Analysis

With the rapid development of the web, cross border investigative processes are literally assaulted and overwhelmed by huge quantities of data. To process and understand these data, due diligence personnel, and investigators must make use of software and web tools. To chart and track down potential criminal enterprises, one can use software applications such as Mindjet* or IBM's I2.[†]

While Mindjet is more generic for brainstorming data, I2 provides intelligence analysis, law enforcement, and fraud investigation solutions, delivering flexible capabilities that help combat crime, terrorism, and fraudulent activity. Jay Liebowitz's book on information analysis, *Strategic Intelligence: Business Intelligence, Competitive Intelligence, and Knowledge Management*[‡] describes I2's use in cases of major investigations on prescription-drug-diversion fraud and other scenarios. I2, Pajek[§], UCInet[¶] and similar software are ultimate tools for cross-border investigative tasks and will provide new value to the due diligence process when trading abroad.

The European Business Registry (EBR) database[**] is another very efficient tool for due diligence process in attempting to prevent an investor in dealing with a corrupt organization abroad. The database, depicted in Figure 4.8, has unified data contained in registries of commerce in Austria, Belgium, Denmark, Estonia, Finland, France, Germany, Greece, Ireland, Italy, Jersey, Latvia, Netherlands, Norway, Serbia, Spain, Sweden, Ukraine, and UK. Name-based searches are possible. Prices differ from country to country and are mentioned with each search.

---

* www.mindjet.com.
[†] http://www-01.ibm.com/software/info/i2software/
[‡] Auerbach Publications (2006).
[§] Pajek, a Slovene word for Spider, is a program for analysis and visualization of large networks. It is freely available, for noncommercial use, at its download page at http://pajek.imfm.si/doku.php?id=download.
[¶] UCINET is a software for analyzing social network data.
[**] http://www.ebr.org.

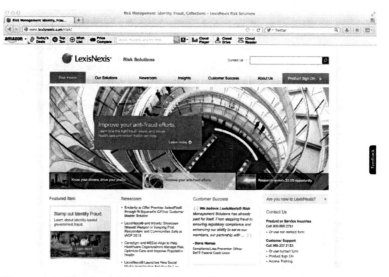

Figure 4.8 *The european business registry database unifies registries of commerce from several european countries*

Source: EBR

Figure 4.9 *The LexisNexis database offers access to media reports, company registrars in many countries, court cases, financial markets information, people's searches and many others*

Another excellent software application is Lexis-Nexis,* as depicted in Figure 4.9. It requires subscription and payment. Lexis-Nexis is a compilation of databases and offers access to media reports, company registrars in many countries, court cases, financial markets information, people's searches, and many others. One useful tool inside Lexis-Nexis is the

---

* http://www.lexisnexis.com/risk/

access to the Dun and Bradstreet companies' database, which covers the whole world. Usually companies involved in imports-exports are listed in this database.

The United States has a wealth of databases, which can be used to track down suspicious corporations. A useful web portal is the National Association of Secretaries of State (NASS) at http://www.nass.org. You will need to register with the portal, free of charge, in order to have access to the registrar of companies of 50 states plus the District of Columbia.

Another good resource is the Global Legal Information Network (GLIN), at http://www.glin.gov, which is a public database of laws, regulations, judicial decisions, and other complementary legal sources contributed by governmental agencies and international organizations. You can find in it data on Paraguay-based companies, published by official publications such as the *Gaceta Oficial de la Republica del Paraguay*.

There are many other resources to assist an investor or organization in conducting a sound due diligence regarding a foreign company. These listed here are just a few of the many resources available, which are beyond the scope of this chapter and book.

Conclusion

The support of international agencies in curbing corruption indicates heightened awareness in the public sector and growing concern on the part of governments to put in place structures and programs dealing with this formidable problem. The increasing concern about the dangers of corruption among the emerging markets, often by multinational corporations from advanced economies, and the need for urgent action must be matched by a similar sense of urgency in the G-7 and G-20 summits. In the final analysis, the political will to empower and support those whose task it is to discover, investigate, reveal, and punish corporations in the public sector will be the major determinant of success. Support from these summits could assist in that regard.

In our opinion, the international business community should work more closely with law enforcement to detect patterns and methods of organized crime, since so many crimes fund terrorism. More detailed analysis of the operation of illicit activities around the world would help advance an understanding of wide spread corruption, crime, and terrorist financing. Corruption overseas, which is so often linked to facilitating organized crime and terrorism, should be elevated to a U.S. national security concern with an operational focus. A joint task force composed of analysts from the Federal Bureau of Investigation (FBI), Department of Homeland Security (DHS), and the Central Intelligence Agency (CIA), as well as Interpol, should be formed to create an integrated system for data collection and analysis. A broader view of today's terrorist and criminal groups is needed, given that their methods and their motives are often shared.

CHAPTER 5

Coping With the Global and Emerging Market Crisis

Overview

After years of robust global economic growth, the implosion in advanced economy financial centers quickly began to negatively affect emerging market economies. Financial markets froze in the aftermath of the Lehman bankruptcy in September 2008 and the emerging markets faced an externally driven collapse in trade and pronounced financial volatility, magnified by deleveraging by banks worldwide further aggravated the situation. As a result, growth of the global economy fell six percent from its precrisis peak to its trough in 2009, the largest straight fall in global growth in the post-war era.

The global crisis had a pronounced but diverse impact on emerging markets. Overall, real output in these countries fell almost four percent between the third quarter of 2008 and the first quarter of 2009, which was the most intense period of the crisis. This average performance, however, masked considerable variation across emerging economies. While real output contracted 11 percent during that period, the worst affected quarter for emerging markets, this was true mostly in emerging Europe only, as output rose one percent during the same period in other less affected emerging market regions, such as with the BRICS.

Emerging markets are still being confronted with two major factors as a result of the global financial crisis, as depicted in Figure 5.1, which include a sudden halt of capital inflows (FDI) driven by a massive global deleveraging, mostly from advanced economies, and a huge collapse in export demand associated with the global slump. Although some emerging markets were already predisposed for a homegrown crisis following

(a)   Net private capital flows (In percent of GDP)

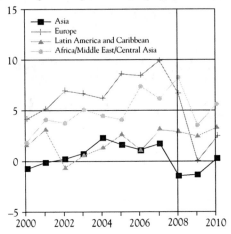

(b)   Exports of goods and services (In percent of GDP)

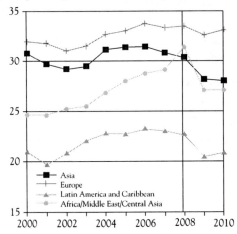

Figure 5.1 Impact of world economic crisis on emerging markets

Source: IMF[1]

unsustainable credit booms or fiscal policies, and faced large debt over-hangs, the majority were not expecting the downturn and have been absorbing the hit from the unwelcome vantage point of surprise.

Earlier this year, in January 2014, emerging markets experienced the worst selloff in currencies in the past five years due to the Federal Reserve's tapering of monetary stimulus, compounded by political and financial instability. The Turkish lira plunged to a record low and South Africa's rand also fell to a level weaker than 11 per dollar for the first time since 2008. Argentine policy makers had to devalue the peso by reducing support in the foreign-exchange market, allowing the currency to drop the most in 12 years to an unprecedented low.

International business professionals and multinationals, as well as investors (in particular) are losing confidence in some of the biggest emerging nations, extending the currency-market rout triggered last year when the U.S. Federal Reserve first indicated it would scale back stimulus. Most financial analysts believe that while Brazil, Russia, India, China, and South Africa were the engines of global growth following the financial crisis in 2008, emerging markets now pose a threat to world financial stability.

We believe, however, emerging markets will continue to grow at much higher rates than advanced economies, but not without pain and financial crises. The current emerging markets exodus isn't like the last crisis in 1997–1998. Back then, emerging market governments borrowed heavily in dollars. When their currencies plunged, they had trouble paying their creditors. And while that scenario is still a concern for some countries, the majority of emerging market debt today is issued in local currency, and many do not owe as much as they did. In our view, analysts and commentators are still suffering from post-2008 financial shock. Despite the facile comparisons, emerging markets are not in as bad a shape as they were in 1997. According to *The Economist,** only two emerging markets out of the 25 the magazine tracks have current account deficits of 5 percent GDP or more. Collectively, emerging markets boast foreign reserves of $7.7 trillion. China alone has, $3.7 trillion.

We also believe the vast majority of analyst commentary, especially those coming out of advanced economies, in particularly the United States, EU, and UK, miss the underlying reasons for emerging market currency volatility, with the yuan being the latest example. In our views, what we're really witnessing is a major rebalancing of global economic trade. Prior to 2008, the United States had a massive consumption bubble, financed by its current account deficit which exported U.S. dollars

---

* http://www.nasdaq.com/article/the-global-guru-heres-why-the-emerging-markets-crisis-of-2014-is-a-red-herring-cm323946#ixzz358xbDGgR

and fueled global trade. Since the crisis, U.S. consumption has slowed but QE has stepped in to provide the U.S. dollar liquidity needed for world trade. With the tapering of QE, that dollar liquidity is diminishing, and emerging market currencies such as the yuan need to adjust to reflect real U.S. demand. Regardless of what the People's Bank of China (PBOC), the central bank of China, does, whether it intervenes or not, this situation was bound to happen. But even if emerging markets were to get hit, they will not necessarily take the rest of the world down with them.

The concern for emerging markets, however, is that this isn't just a currency issue. The carry trades and subsequent inflows of capital have created substantial credit and real estate bubbles in many of these markets. The unwinding of these bubbles is likely to lead to banking crises in several countries, including China and China proxies such as Hong Kong, Australia, and perhaps even Singapore. We do not think this is likely to happen though. If it does, its impact on global economic activity will hurt inflated stock markets and commodity prices, particularly the likes of iron ore and copper which have been widely used as collateral to finance trades and purchases in China. In such case, the outcomes may be very favorable to the United States and the dollar, given less dollar liquidity means reduced supply vis-a-vis demand, as well as U.S. Treasuries, due to the deflationary consequences of the economic rebalancing.

As of 2014 emerging markets account for more than 50 percent of global GDP. Moreover, emerging markets, except for China, represent a third of global imports. If China is included, these markets account for 43 percent of imports. Hence, any slowdown in emerging markets will hurt their imports and therefore exporters in the developed world, including advanced economies. Furthermore, the profits of the United States and many European companies depend on overseas markets, particularly from emerging markets. According to Forbes, as of March 2014, more than 50 percent of U.S. Standards & Poor's (S&P 500) profits are generated outside of the U.S.*

---

* http://www.forbes.com/sites/jamesgruber/2014/03/02/em-banking-crises-are-next/

Advanced Economies Challenges

To make matters worse for emerging markets, advanced economies (G-7) are in a much worse economic situation. The G-7 economies and industrialized economies are struggling with debt and slow growth, which continue to impair its ability to trade and invest with emerging markets. Although these countries represent about 50 percent of world GDP, which totals around $30 trillion dollars, these countries also have a total debt of $140 trillion dollars, a remarkable 440 percent of their GDP. In 1998, total debt of the G-7 was $70 trillion dollars, and their GDP was $30 trillion dollars. Since then, total debt in these advanced economies has doubled between 1998 and 2012, from $70 trillion to $140 trillion, and GDP has risen only by $10 trillion.

In the eurozone, recent economic indicators support the idea that the common-currency area will return to moderate growth by 2014. The road to recovery, however, remains fraught with uncertainties, as the strictly economic issues are far more severe. It has been impossible to summon the necessary political will to take the needed steps until and only when the euro economy teeters on the brink of collapse. At each stage, when the markets crack the whip loudly enough, governments respond. But at each stage, the price of the necessary fix rises. Steps that could have resolved the crisis at one point are inadequate months later. At the time of these writings, the euro crisis continues to drag on without any concrete exit strategy. Greece is still a member of EU, along with Spain, Portugal, Italy, and France with varying degrees of threat. Germany continues to insist that the euro will survive while resisting bold steps to make it so.

Meanwhile, the relative international inactivity, especially during 2012, was partly due to an unusually large number of leadership changes, especially in East Asia. Most major countries, such as Russia, China, North Korea, South Korea, and Japan have witnessed changes of governments and heads of state. While political changes can be breathtakingly swift in the current global landscape, resolving or finding answers to complex economic challenges take time. During this slow economic recovery process, advanced economies have incurred $70 trillion additional debt to produce $10 trillion of additional GDP.

In other words, the world's richest economies are coping with a market crisis where it needs $7 of debt to produce $1 of GDP. Furthermore, for every one percent increase in the borrowing interest rate in its debt, the G-7 adds a staggering $1.4 trillion dollars in debt, undeniably a massive amount of debt. Consider the fact that $1.4 trillion is only slightly less than the entire GDP of Canada. Should interest rates increase by 10 percent, these countries will be looking at an increase in interest expense that equals the entire GDP of the United States.

Some economic sources, policymakers and particularly the media have been suggesting that the G-7 economies, predominantly the eurozone, are slowly recovering, mainly in the UK. What that country is experiencing, however, in our view, is an expansion of nominal GDP. This is not equivalent to real economic growth, as GDP reflects money and credit being injected into the economy. People incorrectly assume this to be the same. Instead of economic recovery, GDP is reflecting money leaving financial markets, particularly bonds, for less interest-rate sensitive havens, which may benefit emerging markets, but has the effect of a double-edge sword. Globally, bonds represent invested capital of over $150 trillion, or more than twice the global GDP. Therefore, even marginal amounts released by rising bond yields can be financially destabilizing, and the effect on GDP growth could be significant.

It is our belief that the mistake of confusing economic progress, a better description of what global markets desire, with GDP is about to show its ugly side, pressuring interest rates to rise early and dragged up by rising bond yields. Take the United States for example, where personal credit in the form of car and student loans has been growing exponentially. The U.S. debt crisis is going up by at least $1 trillion every year. In addition, the U.S. Federal Reserve continues to expand its balance sheet by another $1 trillion each year, which means the U.S. government is currently printing $2 trillion dollars per year. At this pace, unless policymakers change course, we believe the country, and the world economy, will enter a more significant deterioration beginning in 2014. Under such scenario, which we hope won't happen, the United States could be forced to borrow even more, and the Federal Reserve's balance sheet would need to expand by several trillions of dollars.

Eventually it might be much more impactful than that, as in addition to the trillions of dollars of debt, the dollar likely will continue to fall, interest rates will rise, and a hyperinflationary economy starts. Meanwhile, prolonged negotiations in the United States, the largest economy and buyer in the world, regarding the country's debt ceiling have increased uncertainty over its economic growth and that in turn is contributing further to dampening of the global economic growth.

The implosion of the U.S. debt will be extremely unpleasant for the world, particularly for those emerging markets that still rely on the U.S. imports, as well as those trading with other advanced economies invested in the United States. The authors, with sober judgment and concern, anticipate a very difficult time for advanced economies and emerging markets that may extend from 2014 through 2018 and beyond. They believe it will take a very long time for this debt accumulated by the G-7 countries to unwind and for the growth to recover.

It is critical, therefore, that emerging economies develop a credible exit strategy. IMF-like fund may be a good start for BRICS and other similar blocks such as ASEAN, MENA, and CIVETS trading with it, but monetary policy in these emerging countries should not be loosened too quickly, as a rapid reversal would just exacerbate the global *currency wars** already at play and damage credibility for these countries.

The same holds true for fiscal policy interventions, where the stimulus should not be withdrawn too soon and not without a credible exit strategy that places government finances on long-term sustainable footing and helps contain the costs of financing the short-term stimulus. Such an exit strategy would bestow the benefit of strengthening investor confidence and facilitating the resumption of FDI inflows during the recovery phase.

The problem facing G-7 central planners is that a predominantly financial community that has the money to invest in capital assets, such as housing, automobiles, and other luxury items, drives the GDP whimsy. The vast majority of economic stakeholders comprising of pensioners, low-wage workers living from payday to payday, and the unemployed are

---

* Paraphrasing James Richards in his book Currency Wars: The Making of the Next Global Crisis, Portfolio Trade, 2012.

simply disadvantaged as prices, already often beyond their reach, become even more unaffordable. It is a misfortune encapsulated in the concept of the Pareto Principal, otherwise known as the 80/20 rule. The substantial majority will be badly squeezed by rising prices generated by the spending of the few. Global markets are blithely assuming that advanced economies' central banks are in control of events!

Unfortunately, the authors believe central banks are not even in control of their own governments' profligacy, and they are losing their control over markets as well, as the tapering episode shows. In the authors' view, the destructive error of rescuing both the banking system and government finances by heedless currency inflation is in the process of becoming more apparent. Unless this policy is reversed, the world risks a rerun of the collapse of the German mark witnessed in 1923. The printing of money will not positively contribute to long-term economic revival.

The central banks' policies have caused debt to expand exponentially. This has greatly enhanced the economic power of the wealthy, and given the masses the illusion that they are better off, when all they have is a massive debt that can never be repaid. If we just look at the richest one percent in the United States, they have an average of 20 percent debt compared to 80 percent assets. But the masses, 80 percent of the people, have in comparison 90 percent vis-à-vis assets. This, of course, does not include government debt, which is also the people's debt.

For decades, the United States and Europe have been the two centers of global governance. They have, on one hand the ability and experience in international problem solving and, on the other, both the energy and the will to act. All these are assets only when centers of global governance deploy them successfully. Once their model fails, the world will look elsewhere for leadership. At least in the foreseeable future, it will not find any substitutes. Hence, we argue that in the coming years, the United States and China will have to separate rhetoric and fear of the other from actual changes in global policy.

For instance, Stephen Ambrose[2] already pointed out such foreign policy issues in his book *Rise to Globalism*. The author, while seeming to have a serious distaste for the U.S. Presidents Reagan and Johnson, believes Carter was an ideological senseless President that ended up doing the exact opposite of everything he stood for. While holding President

Kennedy as naive and being led/misled by the people around him, the author seems to have the most admiration for Nixon, not as a person, but as a president. He felt Nixon's administration was probably most up to the task of running a super-power.

For instance, a simmering conflict in the East China Sea will have to be managed through and beyond Japan's elections. The United States will have to undo the damage wrought by its announced "Pivot to Asia." The underlying message is that the U.S. is planning to increase its military presence in the region for the purpose of containing China and forcing Asian countries to choose between allying themselves with one or the other great power. It will take much time to convince China that the U.S.' actual intent was, and is, to rebalance its attention from the Middle East toward East Asia, given that the United States has always attempted to exercise its power in Asian with diverse economic, political, and security interests there.

Emerging and Frontier Market Challenges and Opportunities

As discussed throughout this book, emerging markets have been on an inexorable rise over the past decade. During that period, the BRICS powered the high growth rate in emerging market economies, volatility notwithstanding. The rally, however, has started to trickle down in recent years, and came to a screeching halt in 2013, mainly due to fears of U.S. Federal Reserve tapering the stimulus and the slowdown of the Chinese economy.

It is important to note, however, that emerging markets entered the global crisis with varying economic maturity levels and conditions, and thus they are being impacted by the global financial crisis in diverse degrees. Some were already dealing with the beginnings of their own internal economic crisis associated with the end of unsustainable credit booms or fiscal policies, which left in their wake high levels of debt caused mainly by unhedged foreign currency exchange, which will probably require restructuring and perhaps write-offs. Other emerging countries were just caught up in the crash.

A number of emerging economies had to turn to the IMF for financial support. Increases in lending resources, as well as reforms to the lending framework enabled the IMF to quickly react to global developments and put in place 24 arrangements, many with exceptional access, including the recently introduced Flexible Credit Line.* Other countries, many of them highlighted by Jim O'Neil in 2005, dubbed the Next 11, are poised to embark on rapid growth. Many of these countries have matured, improved their economic and trading policies, strengthened their institutions, achieved greater global credibility, and, in many cases, hoarded substantial war chests of foreign exchange reserves.

Progress, however, has not been across the board, with monetary and fiscal policies, FDI flow imbalances, and stock vulnerabilities, varying widely across these emerging economies. Emerging markets are not in "crisis,"; in fact, their growth outpaces that of the United States, Europe, and Japan. But there are many other emerging markets—such as the "frontier" states—that are performing very well economically and deserve attention.

Despite the slowdown of leading emerging markets, these breed of countries, often referred to, as "frontier" markets due to their small, unpopular, and illiquid economies, are prone for fast growth as well. Although these countries have not yet joined the global investment community, they have already joined the global economic community.

Lawrence Speidell[†] argued that the United States as the leading economy in the world as measured by both capitalization and trading volume, was a frontier market in 1792. At the time, the Buttonwood Agreement was executed at an outdoor location, under a buttonwood tree in New York City. It required brokers to trade only with each other and to fix commission rates. China was a frontier market by the late 70's and early 80's, and today, it is the second largest economy in the world, although it is classified as an emerging market.

---

* The Flexible Credit Line (FCL) was designed to meet the increased demand for crisis-prevention and crisis-mitigation lending for countries with very strong policy frameworks and track records in economic performance. To date, three countries, Poland, Mexico and Colombia, have accessed the FCL: due in part to the favorable market reaction, none of the three countries have so far drawn on FCL resources. http://www.imf.org/external/np/exr/facts/fcl.htm.

† Speidell, Lawrence (2011-05-13). Frontier Market Equity Investing: Finding the Winners of the Future (Kindle Locations 67-68). CFA Institute. Kindle Edition.

The same was true for Argentina, once a frontier market, but by 1896, it was about three-quarters as prosperous as the United States and had one of the world's leading stock markets. The country's long decline, at least in relative standing, resulted in purchasing power parity GDP per capita in 2002 that was only double the 1896 level, whereas the United States grew sevenfold over the same period. Even though Argentina has enjoyed a strong recovery and is a solidly middle-income economy, as of this writing, its equity market is still classified as a frontier market because of capital controls that were imposed in 2005. In 2011, the country was in the process of removing these controls, but in 2013 and 2014 much of its progress was derailed, and inflation is accelerating and projected to hit 40 percent in 2014. Nonetheless, most frontier markets are more developed than we think, and set for fast economic growth.

Frontier markets are sometimes referred to as "pre-emerging markets." These are countries with equity markets that are less established, such as Argentina, Kuwait, and Bangladesh. They tend to be characterized by lower market capitalization, less liquidity and, in some cases, earlier stages of economic development. But such markets are not just growth markets in distant places they represent more than 1.2 billion people. These emerging and frontier countries are also placing increasing demands on the world's resources, as they become intensive consumers of basic commodities to support their infrastructure development and manufacturing. In the 1950s, the U.S. Interstate Highway System was built, and China is building its equivalent now. This trend is echoed in railway construction, power plant construction, and new building and bridge construction. It is not just China either. Developing countries around the world are undertaking such projects.

For several decades, frontier markets have been caught in a vicious circle of poverty, with little ability to develop savings for investment in future growth. What investment occurred in frontier countries was done by colonial powers that took out more than they put in. Foreign direct investment (FDI) is highly correlated with GDP growth and can be used as a measure of how the developing economies are faring in globalization. As FDI inflows increase in these markets, we believe that the frontier market growth opportunity is similar in many ways to the opportunity that existed 20 years ago for emerging markets, especially taking into

Country	Rank	Resource
Algeria	6	Barite
Algeria	1	Lead
Algeria	1	Zinc
Armenia	6	Molybdenum
Armenia	2	Rhenium
Botswana	8	Copper
Botswana	2	Diamonds
Botswana	15	Nickel
Botswana	2	Soda
Bulgaria	14	Barite
Guinea	1	Bauxite
Guyana	8	Bauxite
Kazakhstan	11	Bauxite
Kazakhstan	8	Bismuth
Kazakhstan	9	Boron

Figure 5.2 Mineral resource ranks for some of the frontier countries

Source: Speidell, Lawrence*

consideration many of the mineral resources these countries have, as depicted in Figure 5.2.

Following is a list of the main frontier and emerging market countries, sorted alphabetically and by GDP growth forecasts over the next five years, based on our own research and careful observations of economic data, political stability, and infrastructure challenges. Keep in mind that some measures in certain countries are mere estimates as real data may be lacking, and these estimates may vary considerably depending on our sources and timing. Progress has not been across the board though, as monetary and fiscal policies, imbalances in foreign direct investment, and stock vulnerabilities vary widely. This situation is aggravated by the fact that the media tend to emphasize news of conflicts, violence, drought, flood, and human suffering in frontier markets, shifting public opinion

---

* Speidell, Lawrence (2011-05-13). Frontier Market Equity Investing: Finding the Winners of the Future (Kindle Locations 612-615). CFA Institute. Kindle Edition.

against them. Behaviors such as that of Robert Mugabe, president of Zimbabwe, who allowed inflation to reach an absurd 231,000,000 percent in 2008 is an example of news that fosters a general prejudice. But each country should be judged on its own merits.

Highlights of Some Frontier Markets

There are significant opportunities in frontier markets, especially considering their solid capital bases, young labor pool, and improving productivity, particularly in Africa, where the sub-Saharan region will, eventually, overtake China and India. It's plausible to assume that Africa's economy will grow from $2 trillion to $29 trillion by 2050, greater than the current economic output of both the United States and the Eurozone. But we must consider the frontier market's deepening economic ties to China, which makes it vulnerable to a slowing Chinese economy. Also, frontier markets are not without risks, as local politics are complex, and there are still several pockets of corruption and instability. Further, liquidity is scarce, transaction costs can be steep, and currency risk is real. There's also the risk of nationalization of industries.

Bangladesh

Bangladesh is a country the size of the state of Iowa in the United States. It is situated in the northeastern corner of the Indian subcontinent, and bordered by India and Burma. Although geographically small, in reality Bangladesh is a moderate, secular, and democratic country with a population of 160 million, making it the seventh most populous country in the world; notably more populous than Russia. Bangladesh is a big potential market for foreign investors, with a growing garment industry that supports steady export-led economic growth. The country is densely populated, with a rapidly developing market-based economy. Bangladesh is a major exporter of textiles and seafood, with the United States as its largest trading partner. Financial markets are still in their infancy, and thus present a major challenge for growth.

Bangladesh will soon attain lower-middle income status of over $1,036 GDP per capita, thanks to consistent annual GDP average growth of six percent since the 1990s. Much of this growth continues to be driven by the $20 billion garment industry, second only to China, and continued remittance inflows, topping $16 billion in 2013. In 2012, Bangladesh's GDP reached $123 billion, complemented by sound fiscal policy and low inflation, which measured less than 10 percent in 2012.

Bangladesh offers promising opportunities for investment, especially in the energy, pharmaceutical, and information technology sectors as well as in labor-intensive industries. The government of Bangladesh actively seeks foreign investment, particularly in energy and infrastructure projects, and offers a range of investment incentives under its industrial policy and export-oriented growth strategy, with few formal distinctions between foreign and domestic private investors. Bangladesh has among the lowest wage rates in the world, which has fueled an expanding industrial base led by its ready-made garment industry. The country is well-positioned to expand on its success in ready-made garments, diversify its exports, and move up the value chain.

Egypt

As discussed in earlier chapters, Egypt has being politically unstable as a result of the Arab Spring that spread through the Middle East. This political uncertainty has caused massive damage to the economy. Egypt, the third largest economy in Africa, however remains an important emerging market in the region, and the substantial revenues from the Suez Canal, which it controls, makes it even more significant.

Furthermore, Egypt's ability to withstand the financial burden of the revolution, for now at least, was helped by the remarkable growth it posted until December 2011. A financial reform program that began in 2003 had also helped create a well-capitalized and well-managed banking system. For Egypt's economy to revitalize, however, much will depend on how the political process evolves over the coming months. Private-sector investment, which is important for meeting the job creation needs of the country, is currently on hold.

Indonesia

Indonesia is the fourth-largest country in the world by population. Not only it is a G-20 economy, but also the country has a significant and growing middle class with a society that is transitioning to a democracy. The country has relatively low inflation and government debt, and is rich in natural resources including oil, gas, metals, and minerals. Recently, with the fall of its currency, the rupiah, exports received a boost.

While advanced economies were slowing down and many emerging countries were experiencing slowdowns and *exported** financial crisis, Indonesia with a large domestic market and less reliance on international trade, grew through the global financial crisis. Domestic demand constituted the bulk of output in Indonesia, about 90 percent of real GDP in 2007.

Many other emerging markets that also either grew through the crisis or experienced relatively small adverse impact had large domestic markets, such as in China, Egypt, and India. Indonesia also benefited from increased spending associated with national elections in 2009. Hence, Indonesia is recovering faster than many other emerging countries, in part due to a well-timed stimulus. From the first through the last quarters of 2009, output grew 4.5 percent, well above the emerging market's average of 3 percent for the same period. Fiscal stimulus was a step ahead of the curve. As the global economic crisis struck, the government topped up the existing fiscal loosening with cash transfers and other social spending to protect the poor and support domestic demand. The monetary policy response and liquidity management by Bank Indonesia also supported the recovery.

Iran

Although one of the largest oil exporters in the world, Iran's economy is unique as 30 percent of the government, spending goes to religious organizations, which is a major challenge for achieving sustainable growth. The other challenges include administrative controls and widespread corruption and these outweigh positive factors such as a younger, better-educated population, and rapid industrialization. Yet another challenge is the constant risk of economic sanctions and military conflicts. As long as Iran remains committed to supporting terrorism and its nuclear

bullet challenges

---

* Exported financial crisis from advanced economies, and devaluation of those currencies caused inflation in these countries due to hot money inflows.

weapons program, any foreign direct investment opportunity will continue to remain unrealistic.

The United States and EU sanctions targeting Iran's oil exports have hit the country harder than earlier measures, as these financial sanctions have seriously disrupted Iran's trade, for which government authorities were ill prepared. As of fall 2013, Iran was still trying to figure out how to cope with a currency crisis and higher inflation.

Since sanctions were imposed, the rial has fallen to record lows against the U.S. dollar with some reports suggesting it had lost more than 80 percent of its value. The sanctions have slashed Iran's oil exports to around one million barrels a day (b/d). As tensions have increased over Iran's controversial nuclear program, with the United States leading a campaign to undermine the country's economy for coercing the leadership to rescind its policies, the authorities in Tehran have become more secretive over economic data.

Nigeria

As the largest African nation by population, Nigeria is projected to experience high GDP growth rate in the next few years and perhaps for the next several decades. Oil and agriculture account for more than 50 percent of the country's GDP, while petroleum products account for 95 percent of exports. The industrial and the service sectors also are growing. This economic growth potential spurs significant FDI initiatives, mostly from China, the United States, and India. The challenge, however, is with its legal framework and financial markets regulations, which leave much to be desired.

Pakistan

As another frontier market, we believe Pakistan has potential for growth based on its growing population and middle class, rapid urbanization and industrialization, and ongoing, albeit slow, economic reforms. Pakistan has experienced significant growth for several decades. From 1952 until 2013, Pakistan's GDP growth rate has averaged 4.9 percent, reaching an all-time high of 10.2 percent in June of 1954 and a record low of

−1.8 percent in June of 1952. Since 2005 the GDP has been growing at an average of five percent a year, although such growth is not enough to keep up with its fast population growth. Its GDP expanded 3.59 percent from 2012 to 2013.* According to the World Bank,[3] the Pakistani government has made substantial economic reforms since 2000, and medium-term prospects for job creation and poverty reduction are at their best in nearly a decade.

Pakistan's hard currency reserves have grown rapidly. Improved fiscal management, greater transparency and other governance reforms have led to upgrading of Pakistan's credit rating. Together with the prevailing lower global interest rates, these factors have enabled Pakistan to prepay, refinance and reschedule its debts to its advantage. Despite the country's current account surplus and increased exports in recent years, Pakistan still has a large merchandise-trade deficit. The budget deficit in fiscal year 1996–1997 was 6.4 percent of GDP. The budget deficit in fiscal year 2013–2014 is expected to be around four percent of GDP.

In the late 1990s Pakistan received roughly $2.5 billion dollars per year in loan/grant assistance from international financial institutions such as the IMF, the World Bank, and the Asian Development Bank (ADB).[4] Increasingly, however, the composition of assistance to Pakistan shifted away from grants toward loans repayable in foreign exchange. All new U.S. economic assistance to Pakistan was suspended after October 1990, and additional sanctions were imposed after Pakistan's May 1998 nuclear weapons tests. The sanctions were lifted by President George W. Bush after Pakistani President Musharraf allied Pakistan with the United States in its war on terror. Having improved its finances, the government refused further IMF assistance, and consequently ended the IMF program.[5]

Despite such positive GDP growth, Pakistan is still one of the poorest and least developed countries in Asia, with a growing semi-industrialized economy that relies on manufacturing, agriculture, and remittances. To make things worse, political instability, widespread corruption and lack of law enforcement hamper private investment and foreign aid.

---

* http://www.tradingeconomics.com/pakistan/gdp-growth (last accessed on 03/23/2012).

Ahmed Rashid, an investigative journalist with the Daily Telegraph in Lahore,* exposes many facets of Pakistan's political instability in his book titled *Pakistan on the Brink*,[6] where he argues that the bets the U.S. administration has made on trusting Pakistan to support its war efforts in destroying Al Qaeda were not working. Pakistani Taliban, for instance, while pursuing terrorism within Pakistan, has killed more than 1,000 traditional tribal leaders friendly to the Pakistan State, and views the state as an enemy due to its tacit support to U.S. drone attacks. The Taliban's aim, according to Rashid, was, and still is, to establish an Islamic caliphate[†] ignoring political borders.[7]

Pakistan's political framework, Rashid contends, continues to be dominated by its army. Hence, civil government is weak, corrupt and powerless. Apart from the ruling Pakistan Peoples Party[‡] (PPP) there is no other national party, as all other parties are either ethnic or regional, making democracy difficult in a society where the 60 percent Punjab population dominates civil service and the army; others feel underprivileged. Pakistan's political elite has failed to create a national identity that unifies the country. The army's anti-India security paradigm has filled the void to define national identity making the army the most important component of the country.

According to the Asian Development Bank[8] (ADB), the new government that took office in June 2013, however, quickly signaled restoring economic sustainability and rapid growth as high priorities for its five-year term. It emphasized focus on the energy crisis, boosting investment and trade, upgrading infrastructure, and ceding most economic functions to the private sector. To address low foreign exchange reserves, fiscal and external imbalances, and low growth, the government agreed on a wide ranging economic reform program with the IMF, supported by a three-year loan worth $6.7 billion dollars.

---

* Lahore is the capital of the Pakistani province of Punjab and the second largest and metropolitan city in Pakistan.

† A caliphate is an Islamic state led by a supreme religious as well as political leader known as a caliph (meaning literally a successor, i.e., a successor to Islamic prophet Muhammad) and all the Prophets of Islam.

‡ Pakistan People's Party is a center-left, progressive, and social democratic political party in Pakistan.

The program aims to eliminate power subsidies in fiscal consolidation that include strengthening the country's notorious weak revenue base and ending the drain from debt-producing public enterprises. Other structural reforms hope to strengthen the financial system and improve the business climate. ADB* contends that fiscal consolidation would limit GDP growth in 2014 to 3 percent. The current account deficit forecast remains at 0.8 percent of GDP, as the foreign reserve position strengthens. The monetary program is likely to limit average inflation to 8 percent for 2014.

Philippines

The Philippines has shown strong economic progress in the past few years, as shown in Figure 5.3, posting the highest GDP growth rates in Asia during the first two consecutive quarters in 2013. The country weathered the global economic crises very well owed to significant progress made in recent years on fiscal consolidation and financial sector reforms, which contributed to a marked turnaround in investor sentiment, fostering significant FDI inflows.

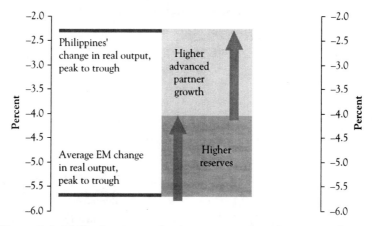

Figure 5.3 Philippines' contributions to growth performance relative to average emerging market growth

Source: Haver; Bloomberg; IMF[9]

---

* Ibidem.

The government used this opportunity of increased FDI inflows to build reserve buffers while keeping exchange rate flexible. Hence, the Philippines entered the global financial crisis on the back of significant improvements in external exposures, which afforded them a smaller output.

The challenges, as a newly industrialized country, are that the Philippines is still an economy with a large agricultural sector, although services are beginning to dominate the economy. Much of the industrial sector is based on processing and assembly operations in the manufacturing of electronics and other high-tech components, usually from foreign multinational corporations. As with many emerging markets, the United States remains Philippines largest trading partner.

Turkey

Turkey's economy, much like the Philippines, has been growing at a fast pace, and for much of the same reasons. Rapid industrialization coupled with steady economic reforms has made Turkey an attractive emerging market. In 2013, however, Turkish economy suffered with civil unrest in the summer and the U.S. taper talk. Turkey's economy remains prone for FDI inflows, but it draws its strength from the country's political stability, unique geographical location on the border of Europe and Asia, market maturity, and economic growth potential.

Vietnam

While agriculture still accounts for 20 percent of Vietnam's GDP (rice and coffee remain the most important crops), its industry and service sectors continue to grow. The major challenge is still its authoritarian regime, which causes its economy to be split between state planned and free market sections. In addition, its economy is still volatile, despite much progress, due to relatively high inflation, lack of transparency in government policy, and a dearth of large enterprises.

MENA Challenges

The Middle East continues to be consumed with the political upheavals of the Arab Awakening: Islamists moving from the familiar role of opposition to the far harder job of governing, religious movements being transformed into political parties, the struggle to organize secular parties, the writing of constitutions, and the holding of elections. In the coming years, it seems likely that sectarian strife will become the defining thread of events across the region.

Through decades of otherwise ineffective rule, the Middle East's dictators did manage to keep divisions between Sunnis and Shia under control. The enforced peace first unraveled in Iraq, where the American invasion triggered a sectarian civil war. The political agreements imposed under the U.S. occupation began to unravel after the departure of American forces, and Iraq today looks like a country about to splinter into Kurdish pieces, late into separate Shia and Sunni pieces, in par, due to Iranian Shia influence.

Iran's mullahs are also playing a major role in Syria, where minority Shia rulers are fighting for very existence in a largely Sunni country. Christians, Kurds, and others are also fighting together and extricating from their countrymen. Sunni and Shia governments across the region ship arms and money to like-minded groups, choosing sides in this second sectarian civil war. Only miles from Damascus, Lebanon—always a sectarian tinderbox—tries desperately to hold on to its fragile peace.

In Bahrain, uprisings, brutally repressed by a Sunni government in a Shia-majority country, are also along sectarian lines. When it comes to foreign affairs, poorly chosen words can do lasting damage. The "Pivot to Asia" was one such example; the other was the "Arab Spring," which led many to expect that the upheavals in the Middle East would lead to swift change and resolution. Unlike the end of Soviet rule in Eastern Europe, these are genuine internal revolutions that will take decades to play out.

The challenge for advanced economies, especially the United States and EU, is to develop the necessary strategic tolerance to distinguish between inevitable ups and downs and long-term trends while helping new governments deliver the economic progress they will need for political survival. We believe Egypt's extraordinarily complex political evolution will continue to play out for the next few years. Overall, events there have been encouraging—the discipline of governing has exerted a moderating influence on the Muslim Brotherhood, the military has relinquished a desire to rule, the country has stuck by its agreement with Israel, and political violence is the exception, not the rule.

In Libya, the government will continue to struggle to take back a government's rightful monopoly on the use of force for internal security from well-armed militias, helped by its oil revenues but hampered terribly by the country's complete lack of functional institutions after forty years of Qaddafi's personal rule. Governments in countries where unrest is still below the surface—Jordan, Kuwait, the Gulf emirates, and Morocco—will continue to stall, hoping that the greater legitimacy they enjoy as monarchies will enable them to avoid major protests and, therefore, retain power. Syria, Iraq, and Iran are where fundamental change is most likely in the year ahead.

As of fall 2013, much is in flux in Israel. Prime Minister Benjamin Netanyahu will have to reevaluate his options in light of the outcome of the U.S. election and public opposition to war. Though his political opposition is weak, elections scheduled for January could force adjustments in Israeli policy.

Other Emerging Market Challenges

The major challenges in the Latin American region are the deterioration of its global economic outlook. We expect regional GDP to expand 3 percent in 2014, as there has been a negative trend in growth prospects for Argentina, Chile, Uruguay and Venezuela, although growth prospects for Bolivia and Ecuador are positive. Brazil and Mexico will likely grow at a 2.7 percent, which we believe to be a rebound trend from the nearly uninterrupted negative trend downward that began in June 2012.

The deterioration of some BRICS economies, particularly Russia and India also has contributed to the slowdown of global growth. Within Latin America, we believe Brazil and Mexico will experience growth starting in 2014. In the late summer of 2013 Brazil's economy grew 0.1 percent over the previous month, from a decline of 0.3 percent in July.

Mexico is the second-largest economy in Latin America, following Brazil. The country, which has been on the U.S. FDI radar for some time, is a G-20 member and democracy. Its geographical location and the NAFTA agreement make the United States its largest trading partner. Mexico's low inflation and unemployment add to the economy's promise.

Mexico has been engendering much confidence with both policy reforms and the country's inherent strategic advantages. It is easy to forget just how sizable the economy is. At 14th in the world, ahead of South Korea, Mexico enjoys a balanced government budget, a steadily growing population, a dramatically reduced deficit and relatively high interest rates. The country boasts many large multinational companies, as depicted in Figure 5.4,[10] many of them are listed in the U.S. stock exchanges.

The Mexican economy also is expected to grow, although in this case it is providing mixed signals. The external sector continues to show healthy developments as Mexican exports grew solidly in early fall of 2013. Nonetheless, the manufacturing indicator fell in October 2013 after three consecutive months of improvement. The index is again below the 50-point threshold, which separates expansion from contraction in the manufacturing sector.

While the Mexican government's push for economic reforms promises to boost economic growth in the medium- to long-term, short-term economic headwinds persist amid uncertainty in the U.S. economy, sluggish domestic demand, and a negative weather-related impact. We believe

Rank	Name	Industry	Foreign assets
1	Cemex	Non-metallic minerals	40,334
2	America Movil	Telecommunications	23,610
3	Carso Global Telecom	Telecommunications	11,768
4	Grupo FEMSA	Beverages	3,508
5	Grupo ALFA	Diversified	3,439
6	Grupo México	Mining	2,850
7	PEMEX	Oil & gas	2,090
8	Gruma	Food products	1,986
9	Grupo BIMBO	Food products	1,850
10	Grupo Televisa	Television, motion pictures, radio & telecommunications	1,614
11	Cementos de Chihuahua	Non-metallic minerals	952
12	Industrias CH	Steel & metal products	790
13	Mexichem	Chemicals & petrochemicals	730

Figure 5.4 Ranking of Mexican multinational companies, as of 2008

Source: Columbia University

Mexico is prone to grow 3.5 percent in 2014. Against a backdrop of contained inflationary pressures and sluggish domestic demand, central banks across Latin America must decide whether to lower or maintain interest rates in order to support economic growth. We expect Mexico's central bank to cut interest rates, but not so in Brazil, as the country's central bank is still involved in a tightening cycle.

Led by a collapse in domestic demand, Russia experienced a sharper-than-expected contraction in output during the global economic crisis causing the output to fall sharply by about 11 percent of GDP from its peak. Compared to many other emerging economies, Russia had much lower external vulnerabilities when the crisis started, but the country suffered one of the largest output downfalls in the emerging markets. Oil prices were an important factor in the collapse of Russia's outputs.

As oil prices collapsed in the midst of the global recession, trading partners revised their outlook for the economy and the ruble, causing the domestic demand to plunge due to the immediate change in policies by trading partners. At the same time, capital outflows, banks' increased risk aversion, and an associated credit crunch exacerbated the collapse. High oil prices may have masked inefficiencies in un-restructured sectors.

In addition, a pre-crisis credit boom fueled in part by a rigid exchange rate regime helps explain the eventual impact of the crisis. Through 2007, Russia was growing at seven percent per year on average, driven by high oil prices, expanding domestic demand, and a credit boom. As a result, by the time of the crisis, some corporations and banks had become increasingly reliant on short-term capital flows.

As the crisis unfolded, Russia spent more than $200 billion of its reserves, the equivalent of about 13 percent of its 2008 GDP in an attempt to temper the pressure on the ruble, but eventually the government appeared to given up and allowed for a significant fall in the exchange rate. This was one of the largest declines amongst emerging markets.

Russia's high reserves provided some space for corporates and banks to adjust to a revised global outlook with lower oil prices, and this helped Russia to avoid the crisis from spinning out of control completely. Nevertheless, this had its own costs. Some market participants were able to benefit from speculating on the eventual devaluation, and some of the problem banks will eventually need intermediation to support the recovery.

Conclusion

This chapter ends where it began. Even though the global crisis started in the financial markets of advanced economies, emerging markets suffered a heavy toll. The median emerging market economy suffered about as large a decline in output as the median advanced economy, but the impact was more varied in emerging markets, as depicted in Figure 5.5. Several emerging markets were impacted more than the worst hit advanced economies, while other emerging markets continued to grow throughout the crisis period. While on average emerging markets experienced significant decline in stock markets and as wide span as advanced economies, there was considerable cross-country variability.

Countries with higher pre-crisis vulnerabilities and trade and financial linkages with the global economy, in particular the advanced economies, were more impacted by the crisis. Countries that experienced a decline in vulnerabilities before the crisis came out well ahead of others. One of the

Impact of the crisis		
	Emerging markets	Adduced economies
Output collapse[a]		
Median	−4.3	−4.5
25th percentile	−8.4	−6.6
75th percentile	−2.0	−2.9
Stock market collapse[a]		
Median	−57.1	−55.4
25th percentile	−72.0	−64.1
75th percentile	−45.2	−49.0
Rise in sovereign spreads[b]		
Median	462	465
25th percentile	287	. . .
75th percentile	772	. . .

[a]Measured as percent change from peak to trough.
[b]Measured as increase in basis points lrom trough to peak. For A Es, table reports rise in spreads on US corporates rated BBS.

Figure 5.5 The impact of the global financial crisis on advanced economies and emerging markets

Source: Haver; Bloomberg; IMF

factors that lowered pre-crisis exposure was higher international reserve in relation to short-term external financing needs. Nevertheless, additional reserves were less useful at limiting output collapse at very high levels of reserves.

In our view, no foreign policy issue, in 2014 and beyond, will matter as much for the global economic, political, and ultimately security conditions as the ability or the willingness of the United States and EU to deal decisively with their economic crises. If the United States can find an exit strategy for its "fiscal cliff," the resolution of the acute economic uncertainty would unleash private sector investment, spark an economic recovery, and enhance the country's pivotal international role.

Advanced economies have responded to the crisis through unprecedented monetary and fiscal easing. As for the emerging markets, those in the midst of a homegrown capital account crisis may have to orient their policies toward restoring confidence in the currency, with little scope for easing in either dimension without exacerbating capital outflows. Emerging markets with credible inflation targeting frameworks should have considerable scope for monetary policy easing without compromising their inflation outlooks.

Likewise, the collapsing external demand and weakening domestic economic activity would, in general, call for fiscal easing to support demand, provided debt sustainability is not a concern and financing is available. Given a targeted level of aggregate demand/inflation, a more expansionary monetary policy can compensate for a less expansionary fiscal policy—though both may be relatively ineffective if domestic credit markets are frozen. Substituting for monetary easing by fiscal expansion can be constrained by debt sustainability concerns, because both relatively higher interest rates and fiscal spending will exacerbate debt dynamics.

There is no one-size-fits-all prescription, and the appropriate policy mix depends on the particular circumstances in each country, including a number of trade-offs. For Europe, the world's largest economic entity and a critical leader of a liberal and peaceful world order, the challenge continues to be to summon sustained economic discipline and political will.

Progress has been made. Governments have firmly convinced themselves, if not the markets, that they will do whatever it takes to save the euro. Thanks largely to the efforts of two Italians—Mario Monti, the

Recovery from the Crisis (averages, percent)		
	GDP growth, 2009Q4/2009Q1	Industrial production growth[a]
	(1)	(2)
All EMs	3.1	10.8
By exchange rate regime		
Fixed exchange rate regimes	0.2	−1.6
Flexible exchange rate regimes	3.9	14.0
By region		
Asia	6.4	26.7
Europe	1.2	4.3
MCD	4.8	10.9
Western hemisphere	3.1	9.7

[a]From each country's trough to Dec. 2009.

Figure 5.6 Emerging markets recovery from the global financial crisis

Source: Haver; IMF AREAR; IMF

economist appointed interim prime minister to put Italy's house in order, and Mario Draghi, the new head of the European Central Bank—concrete steps have been taken that show a rescue is possible. But painful structural reforms will have to be endured for many years—a tall order for any one democracy, let alone for many sharing each other's pain. In effect, the euro crisis morphed in 2012 from a life-threatening emergency to a chronic disease that will be with us for years to come. The challenge for 2014–15 is to maintain the harsh treatment, avoid setbacks (in France, especially), and continue to inch toward restored growth.

For emerging markets, recovery was underway in most of the nations by late 2009, with considerable variation across countries. On average, real GDP expanded three percent in emerging markets during the last three quarters of 2009, but as in the impact of the crisis, this masks considerable cross-country variation. For instance, countries not pegging to the dollar, or other advanced economy currency, recovered much faster than those that were pegged. Across emerging market regions, as depicted in Figure 5.6, the recovery was most pronounced in Asia, particularly in the ASEAN bloc, and least in emerging Europe.

About the Authors

Marcus Goncalves, EdD, is an international management consultant with more than 25 years of experience in the United States, Latin America, Europe, Middle East, and Asia. Mr. Goncalves is the former CTO of Virtual Access Networks, which under his leadership was awarded the *Best Enterprise Product* at Comdex Fall 2001, leading to the acquisition of the company by Symantec. He holds a master's degree in Computer Information Systems and a doctorate in Educational Leadership from Boston University. He has more than 45 books published in the United States, many translated into Portuguese, German, Chinese, Korean, Japanese, and Spanish. He's often invited to speak on international business, global trade, international management and organizational development subjects worldwide. Marcus has been lecturing at Boston University and Brandeis University for the past 11 years. He has also been a visiting professor and graduate research adviser/examiner at Saint Joseph University, in Macao, China for the past three years. He is an Associate Professor of Management, and the International Business Program Chair at Nichols College, in Dudley, MA, USA. Dr. Goncalves can be contacted via e-mail at marcus.goncalves@nichols.edu or at marcusg@mgcgusa.com.

José Alves, PhD, is an Associate Professor of Management at the Faculty of Business, Government, and Social Work of the University of Saint Joseph, Macau. He holds a PhD in Business Administration from the University of Massachusetts Amherst. He currently is based in Macau, China, but has lived in Europe and the United States. His major research interests include leadership and management in international contexts, namely in Asia and China. His research has been published in journals and conference proceedings, such as the Journal of Managerial Psychology, Human Resources Management Review, and International Journal of Leadership Studies. He has also presented at various conferences, including the Academy of Management, Iberoamerican Academy of Management, International Association for Chinese Management Research, and

Academy of Human Resource Development. He is an entrepreneur and advisor to European companies intending to enter into Asia and China. Dr. Alves can be contacted via e-mail at jose.alves@usj.edu.mo.

Rajabahadur V. Arcot, MSc Physics, is an Independent Industry Analyst/Columnist and Business Consultant with around 40 years of senior managerial experience. He has held C-level executive positions in leading companies, such as Honeywell, Thermax, Bells Controls an affiliate of Foxboro/Invensys, Electronics Corporation of India Limited and Instrumentation Limited. Until recently, he was responsible for ARC Advisory Group's business operations in India. He has authored and reviewed numerous market research and industry trend reports, white papers, and case studies, widely travelled, transacted business with numerous leading Indian and Fortune 500 transnational companies. He has been a regular contributor to Industry and Industry Association Publications and speaker at numerous conferences and events in India and abroad. Presently, as an Independent Industry Analyst/Columnist and Business Consultant, he focuses on providing consultancy services and writes reports, articles, case studies, and white papers on critical infrastructure industry control systems cyber security, sustainable manufacturing, Industry 4.0 trends, renewable energy and distributed generation, and professional & skill competency development. He is a postgraduate from the University of Mysore and holds MSc degree in physics. Rajabahadur can be contacted at rajabahadurav@gmail.com.

Advance Quotes
for *Doing Business*
in Emerging Markets

The authors did a great job in providing a classical analysis of the international markets. This book is the foundation for the practical implementation of UN programs for development of the world market, the fight against poverty, the fight against unemployment, strengthening the multicultural world and much more. But even more so, this book gives a loud signal to changes in the macroeconomic and monetary policy for the leading countries of the world, and opens up the possibility of the growth rates of major reserve currency of the world. The authors provide clear guidance to all segments of the global and regional business, show the development of new markets, and provide an open understanding of creating a single world economic system and strengthen relations between the States at all levels. Overall development becomes an ambassador of peace and prosperity between the continents. Great work of scientists on a global scale. I recommend this book for professionals of all sectors of business and economists of all interested countries and governments.

—Yurii Pozniak, International Management Consultant
at Ukroboronservis, Kiev, Ukraine

This book provides a complete review about political and economic impacts in developing business abroad. It shows a very interesting historical review with recent facts clearly punctuated. You will enjoy it.

—Osvaldo Costa, Senior HR Manager
at Tigre S.A., Joinville, Santa Catarina, Brazil

This book provides a good review of the challenges facing business in the emerging markets and initiates the discussion of the roadmap necessary for success. I found it thought-provoking and recommend it to anyone with a desire to take their business from local to global.

—Jayshree Pandya, Founder Risk Group LLC
(http://www.riskgroupllc.com) and author of the book,
The Global Age: NGIOA @ Risk

Notes

Chapter 1

1. Mitchell, Jared (2013).
2. The World Bank (2013). (last accessed on 09/22/2012).
3. Mitchell, Jared (2013).
4. The World Bank (2013). (last accessed on 09/22/2012).
5. Pacek, N. (2007).
6. http://globaledge.msu.edu/mpi
7. Cavusgil, S. Tamer (1997).
8. Cavusgil, S. Tamer (2004).
9. Khanna, Tarun (2010).
10. Arkalgud, Arnand Prasad (2011).
11. Mutum, Dilip S. (2014).

Chapter 2

1. Maxwell, John (2012).
2. Kose, M.A. (2012).
3. Bain & Company's Staff Analysts (2012).
4. Bonham, C. (2004).
5. Manyika, J. (2012).
6. Soubbotina, Tatyana P. (2004).
7. http://www.bain.com/publications/articles/a-world-awash-in-money.aspx (last accessed on 12/7/2013).

Chapter 3

1. Al Jazeera Staff Writers (2011a).
2. Abulof, Uriel (2011).
3. Peterson, S. (2011).
4. Spencer, R. (2011).
5. Bakri, N. and D. Goodman (2011).
6. Richter, Frederick (2011).
7. Koelbl, Susanne (2011).
8. Afrol News of Morocco Staff Writers (2011).

9. Aljazeera Staff Writers (2011).

10. Associate Press Staff Writers (2011).

11. Al-Ansary, Khalid (2011).

12. Hauser, Christine (2013).

13. McCrummen, Stephanie (2011).

14. Middle East Online Staff Writers (2011). "Kuwaiti stateless protest for third day."

15. Al Jazeera Staff Writers (2011b).

16. Seyid, Seyid Ould (2011).

17. Corrigan, Terence (2007).

18. Vaidya, Sunil (2011).

19. Nath, Ravindra (2011).

20. BBC News Middle East Staff Writers (2011).

21. Manson, Katrina (2011).

22. Afrol News Staff Writers (2011).

23. Human Rights Watch Staff Writers (2012).

24. Donnison, Jon (2011).

25. Snyder, Michael (2012).

26. Boone, E. (2007).

Chapter 4

1. Transparency International Secretariat (2013).

2. Radu, Paul C. (2008).

3. Rich, Ben R. & Janos, Leo (1994).

4. Amartya Sen (1999).

5. Moore, M. (2005).

6. Freeland, Chrystia (2012).

7. OECD (2007).

8. Posadas, Alejandro (2000).

9. Stout, David (2009).

10. Barstow, David (2012).

11. Welch, D. (2012).

12. Garcia-Palafox, Galia (2012).

13. Hamburger, T. (2012).

14. Crawford, David; Searcey, Dionne (April 16, 2010).

15. BBC News Staff Writers (2011).

16. U.S. Department of Justice (2012).

17. The FCPA Blog (2012).

18. Smith & Nephew (2012).

19. Barrera, C., Dobbyn, T. (2012).

20. New York City Bar Association (2011).
21. Department of Justice (2010).
22. Department of Justice (2011).
23. Dooley, Emily (2010).
24. Carton, Bruce (2011).

Chapter 5

1. Ghosh A.R. (2009).
2. Ambrose, S. and Brinkley, D. (2011)
3. World Bank, (2012). (last accessed 11/10/2012).
4. Cheema, F. (2004).
5. Hoti, Ikram (2004).
6. Rashid, Ahmed (2012), p. 87.
7. Rashid, Ahmed (2012), p. 87.
8. Asian Development Bank (2013).
9. Moghadam, Reza (2010).
10. Vale Columbia Center on Sustainable International Investment (2009).

References

Abulof, Uriel. 2011. "What Is the Arab Third Estate?" *Huffington Post*, http://www.huffingtonpost.com/uriel-abulof/what-is-the-arab-third-es_b_832628.html, (last accessed on 11/12/2013).

Afrol News of Morocco Staff Writers. 2011. "Morocco King on holiday as people consider revolt," *Afrol News*, http://www.afrol.com/articles/37175, (last accessed on 11/01/2013).

Afrol News Staff Writers. 2011. "New clashes in occupied Western Sahara," *Afrol News*, http://www.afrol.com/articles/37450, (last accessed on 10/25/2013).

Ahmed, Masood. 2010. "Trade Competitiveness and Growth MENA," *World Economic Forum's Arab World Competitiveness Review*, http://www.imf.org/external/np/vc/2010/103010.htm, (last accessed on 01/03/2014).

Akhtar, S.I., M.J. Bolle, and R.M. Nelson. 2013. "U.S. Trade and Investment in the Middle East and North Africa: Overview and Issues for Congress," *Congress Research Service*. http://fpc.state.gov/documents/organization/206138.pdf, (last accessed on 7/10/2014).

Al Jazeera Staff Writers. 2011a. "Tunisia's Ben Ali flees amid unrest," *Al Jazeera*, http://www.aljazeera.com/news/africa/2011/01/20111153616298850.html, (last accessed on 11/15/2013).

Al Jazeera Staff Writers. 2011b. "Sudan police clash with protesters," *Al Jazeera*, http://www.aljazeera.com/news/africa/2011/01/2011130131451294670.html, (last accessed on 09/12/2013).

Al Masah Capital Management Limited. 2010. "China and India's Growing Influence in the MENA Region: Their Legacy and Future Footprint." http://s3.amazonaws.com/zanran_storage/ae.zawya.com/ContentPages/142996358.pdf, (last accessed on 01/03/2014).

Al-Ansary, Khalid. 2011. "Iraq's Sadr followers march against Bahrain crackdown," *Reuters*, http://www.reuters.com/article/2011/03/16/us-bahrain-iraq-idUSTRE72F4U220110316, (last accessed on 11/12/2013).

Aljazeera Staff Writers. 2011. "Thousands protest in Jordan," 01/28/2011, *Al Jazeera*, http://www.aljazeera.com/news/middleeast/2011/01/2011128125157509196.html, (last accessed on 10/25/2013).

Amadeo, K. 2013. "What Is a Currency War?" http://useconomy.about.com/od/tradepolicy/g/Currency-Wars.htm, (last accessed on 6/15/2014).

Amartya Sen. 1999. *Development as Freedom*. Oxford, United Kingdom: Oxford University Press.

Ambrose, S. and Brinkley, D. 2011. Rise to Globalism. New York, NY: Penguin Group.

American Chamber of Commerce, International Affairs. 2013. "ASEAN Business Outlook Survey," *Singapore Business Federation*, http://www.amcham.org.sg/wp-content/uploads/2013/08/2014ABOS.pdf, (last accessed on 10/24/2013).

Amin, M. 2009. "Labor Regulation and Employment in India's Retail Stores," *Journal of Comparative Economics*, 37 (1): 47–61.

An Alternative Economic System. Al Jazeera Center for Studies. Retrieved from http://studies.aljazeera.net/en/reports/2013/06/20136474134190632.htm, (last accessed on 12/19/2013).

Arabia Monitor. 2012. "Shifting Sands, Shifting Trade: Building a New Silk Route," *Middle East and North Africa Outlook Q4 2012.* http://www.researchandmarkets.com/reports/2253210/q4_2012_mena_outlook_shifting_sands_shifting, (last accessed on 12/19/2013).

Arkalgud, A.P. 2011. "Filling "institutional voids" in emerging markets," *Forbes.* http://www.forbes.com/sites/infosys/2011/09/20/filling-institutional-voids-in-emerging-markets/

Asian Development Bank. 2013. "Asian Development Outlook 2013 Update," *ADB.* Manila, http://www.adb.org/countries/pakistan/economy, (last accessed on 12/20/2013).

Associate Press Staff Writers. 2011. "Algeria protest draws thousands," *CBC News World/Associate Press.* http://www.cbc.ca/news/world/algeria-protest-draws-thousands-1.1065078, (last accessed on 11/02/2013).

Axworthy, T. 2010. *Who Gets to Rule the World?* Canada: Macleans.

Bain & Company's Staff Analysts. 2012. "A world awash in money," *Bain & Company.* http://www.bain.com/publications/articles/a-world-awash-in-money.aspx, (last accessed on 12/07/2013).

Bakri, N. and D. Goodman. 2011. "Thousands in Yemen Protest against the Government," *The New York Times.* http://www.nytimes.com/2011/01/28/world/middleeast/28yemen.html?_r=0, (last accessed on 11/11/2013).

Barrera, C., and T. Dobbyn. 2012. "U.S. says BizJet settles foreign bribery charges," *Reuters.* http://www.reuters.com/article/2012/03/14/us-mexico-lufthansa-idUSBRE82D1H220120314, (last accessed on 10/28/2013).

Barstow, David. 2012. "Vast Mexican Bribery Case Hushed Up by Wal-Mart After High-Level Struggle," *The New York Times.* http://www.nytimes.com/2012/04/22/business/at-wal-mart-in-mexico-a-bribe-inquiry-silenced.html?_r=0, (last accessed on 05/13/2012).

BBC News Middle East Staff Writers. 2011. "Man dies after setting himself on fire in Saudi Arabia," *BBC News.* http://www.bbc.co.uk/news/world-middle-east-12260465, (last accessed on 11/04/2013).

BBC News Staff Writers. 2011. "News Corp shares hit two-year low on hacking arrest," *BBC World News.* http://www.bbc.co.uk/news/business-14181119, (last accessed on 02/04/2012).

Bhattacharya, R., and H. Wolde. 2010a. "Constraints on Growth in the MENA Region," *IMF Working Papers*, 1–21.

Bhattacharya, R., and H. Wolde. 2010b. "Constraints on Trade in the MENA Region," *IMF Working Papers*, 1–18.

Bishku, Michael B. 2010. "South Africa and the Middle East," *Journal Essay Middle East Policy Council.* Fall 2010, Vol. XVII, No. 3.

Blanchart, Olivier. 2013. "Advanced Economies Strengthening, Emerging Market Economies Weakening," *IMFDirect.* http://blog-imfdirect.imf. org/2013/10/08/advanced-economies-strengthening-emerging-market-economies-weakening/, (last accessed on 10/15/2013).

Blanke, Jennifer. 2013. "The Global Competitiveness Report 2013–2014," *World Economic Forum.* http://www.weforum.org/issues/global-competitiveness, (last accessed on 11/24/2013).

Bonham, C., B. Gangnes, and A.V. Assche. 2004. "Fragmentation and East Asia's Information Technology Trade," *Department of Economics at the University of Hawaii at Manoa, and University of California at Davis.* Working Paper No. 04.09. http://www.economics.hawaii.edu/research/workingpapers/WP_04–9 .pdf, (last accessed on 12/01/2013).

Boone, Elisabeth. 2007. "Political Risk in Emerging Markets," *The Rough Notes Company, Inc.* http://www.roughnotes.com/rnmagazine/2007/october07/10 p060.htm, (last accessed 11/11/2013).

Brahmbhatt, M., O. Canuto, and S. Ghosh. 2010. "Currency Wars Yesterday and Today." *Economic Premise*, 43.

Bremmer, Ian. 2009. *State Capitalism and the Crisis.* Eurasia Group.

Bremmer, Ian. 2013. *Every Nation for Itself: Winners and Losers in a G-zero World.* New York City, NY: Portfolio/Penguin

Bukharin, N. 1972. *Imperialism and World Economy.* London: Merlin.

Business Standard of India Staff Writers. 2011. "BRICS is passé, time now for 3G:Citi," *Business Standard.* New Delhi, India. http://www.business-standard. com/india/news/brics-is-passe-time-now-for-percent5C3gpercent5C-citi/126725/on, (last accessed on 11/01/2013).

Caballero, Ricardo. 2009. "Sudden Financial Arrest." *10th Jacques Polak Annual Research Conference.* http://www.imf.org/external/np/res/seminars/2009/arc/ pdf/caballero.pdf, (last accessed on 11/30/2013).

Cammett, M. 2013. "Development and Underdevelopment in the Middle East and North Africa." In Carol Lancaster and Nicolas van de Walle (eds.), *Handbook of the Politics of Development.* New York, NY: Oxford University Press, 2013 (Forthcoming). Available at SSRN: http://ssrn.com/abstract=2349387, (last accessed on 12/20/2013).

Canuto, O. 2010. "Toward a Switchover of Locomotives in the Global Economy." *Economic Premise*, 33.

Canuto, O. and M. Giugale (Eds). 2010. *The Day After Tomorrow—A Handbook on the Future of Economic Policy in the Developing World*. Washington, DC: World Bank.

Cartas, Jose. 2010. "Dollarization Declines in Latin America, Finance and Development," March 2010, Vol. 47, No. 1. http://www.imf.org/external/pubs/ft/fandd/2010/03/pdf/spot.pdf, (last accessed on 11/05/2013).

Carton, Bruce. 2011. "Company Allegedly Bumped Out of Contract by Rival's Corruption Recovers $45 Million in Civil Settlement," *Compliance Week*. http://www.complianceweek.com/company-allegedly-bumped-out-of-contract-by-rivalscorruption-recovers-45-million-in-civil-settlement/article/213666/, (last accessed on 12/10/2013).

Cashin, P., M.K. Mohaddes, and M.M. Raissi. 2012. "The Global Impact of the Systemic Economies and MENA," *Business Cycles* (Working Paper No. 12–255). International Monetary Fund.

Cavusgil, S. Tamer, Tunga Kiyak, and Sengun Yeniyurt. 2004. "Complementary Approaches to Preliminary Foreign Market Opportunity Assessment: Country Clustering and Country Ranking," *Industrial Marketing Management*, October 2004, Vol. 33(7), pp. 607–617.

Cavusgil, S. Tamer. 1997. "Measuring the Potential of Emerging Markets: An Indexing Approach," *Business Horizons*, January-February 1997, Vol. 40(1), pp. 87–91.

Central Intelligence Agency. 2013. "The World Factbook," https://www.cia.gov/library/publications/the-world-factbook/, (last accessed on 09/23/13).

Cheema, Faisal. 2004. "Macroeconomic Stability of Pakistan: The Role of the IMF and World Bank (1997–2003)," *Programme in Arms Control, Disarmament, and International Security (ACDIS)*. University of Illinois at Urbana-Champaign. http://acdis.illinois.edu/assets/docs/250/MacroeconomicStabilityof PakistanTheRoleoftheIMFandWorldBank19972003.pdf, (last accessed on 12/14/2013).

Cheewatrakoolpong, K., C. Sabhasri, and N. Bunditwattanawong. 2013. "Impact of the ASEAN Economic Community on ASEAN Production Networks," *IDBI*, No. 409. http://www.adbi.org/files/2013.02.21.wp409. impact.asean.production.networks.pdf, (last accessed on 03/12/2013).

Chheang, Vannarith. 2008. "The Political Economy of Tourism in Cambodia," *Asia Pacific Journal of Tourism Research* 13 (3): 281–297. Retrieved 9 February 2013.

China The People's Daily. 2011. "Asia to play bigger role on world stage, G20: ADB report." *The People's Daily*. April 26, 2011. http://english.people. com.cn/90001/90778/98506/7361425.html, (last accessed on 10/01/2013).

Clinton, Hillary. 2011. "America's Pacific Century," *Foreign Policy*. http://www. foreignpolicy.com/articles/2011/10/11/americas_pacific_century, (last accessed on 11/12/2012).

CNN. 2009. "Officials: G-20 to supplant G-8 as international economic council." *CNN*, http://edition.cnn.com/2009/US/09/24/us.g.twenty.summit/, (last accessed on 10/03/2013).

Colombo, Jesse. 2013. "Why The Worst Is Yet To Come For Indonesia's Epic Bubble Economy," *Forbes*. http://www.forbes.com/sites/jessecolombo/2013/10/03/why-the-worst-is-yet-to-come-for-indonesias-epic-bubble-economy/2/, (last accessed on 10/05/2013).

Condon, Stephanie. 2013. "Obama appeals to senators to hold off on more Iran sanctions," *CBSNews*. http://www.cbsnews.com/news/obama-appeals-to-senators-to-hold-off-on-more-iran-sanctions/, (last accessed on 12/19/2013).

Corrigan, Terence. 2007. "Mauritania: Country Made Slavery Illegal last Month," *The East African Standard*. http://www.saiia.org.za/opinion-analysis/mauritania-made-slavery-illegal-last-month, (last accessed on 11/10/2013).

Crawford, David, and Dionne Searcey. 2010. "U.S. Joins H-P Bribery Investigation." *The Wall Street Journal*. http://online.wsj.com/news/articles/SB10001424052702304628704575186151115576646, (last accessed on 12/28/2012).

Daniele, V. and U. Marani. 2006. "Do institutions matter for FDI? A comparative analysis for the MENA countries." *University Library*, Munich, Germany.

Das, Satyajit. 2013. "The new economic nationalism," *ABC Australia*. http://www.abc.net.au/news/2013–09-30/das-the-new-economic-nationalism/4988690, (last accessed on 12/12/2013).

Deen, Ebrahim Shabbir. 2013. "BRICS & Egypt: An Opportunity to Begin Creating an Alternative Economic System." *Al Jazeera Center for Studies*. http://studies.aljazeera.net/en/reports/2013/06/20136474134190632.htm, (last accessed on 12/19/2013).

Department of Justice. 2010. "Innospec Inc. Pleads Guilty to FCPA Charges and Defrauding United Nations; Admits to Violating the U.S. Embargo Against Cuba." http://www.justice.gov/opa/pr/2010/March/10-crm-278.html, (last accessed on 12/10/2013).

Department of Justice. 2011. "Innospec Inc. Pleads Guilty to FCPA Charges and Defrauding United Nations; Admits to Violating the U.S. Embargo Against Cuba." Second Amended Complaint 1, Newmarket Corp. v. Innospec Inc., No. 3:10-cv-00503 (E.D.Va. Jan. 27, 2011) (ECF No. 41).

Dilip S. Mutum, Sanjit Kumar Roy, and Eva Kipnis (eds). 2014. *Marketing Cases from Emerging Markets*. New York, NY: Springer.

Donnison, Jon. 2011. "Palestinians emboldened by Arab Spring," *Ramallah: BBC News*. http://www.bbc.co.uk/news/world-middle-east-13417788, (last accessed on 11/16/2013).

Dooley, Emily C. 2010. "Richmond firm claims in suit that competitor paid kickbacks to Iraqis," *Richmond Times-Dispatch*. B-03.

Dresen, F.J. 2011. "BRICS: Shaping the New Global Architecture," *Woodrow Wilson International Center for Scholars*. http://www.wilsoncenter.org/publication/brics-shaping-the-new-global-architecture, (last accessed on 4/5/2012).

Durand, M., C. Madaschi, and F. Terribile. 1998. "Trends in OECD countries' international competitiveness: the influence of emerging market economies," *OECD Economics Department Working Paper, No. 195*.

Economists Staff Writers. (2013). "The gated globe," *The Economist*. http://www.economist.com/news/special-report/21587384-forward-march-globalisation-has-paused-financial-crisis-giving-way, (last accessed on 11/12/2013).

Economists Staff Writers. 2010. "BRICS and BICIS." *The Economist*. http://www.economist.com/blogs/theworldin2010/2009/11/acronyms_4, (last accessed on 11/9/2012).

Economists Staff Writers. 2012. "And the winner is...." *The Economist*. http://www.economist.com/node/21542926, (last accessed on 12/13/2013).

Economists Staff Writers. 2012. "Gushers and guns," *The Economist*. http://www.economist.com/node/21550304, (last accessed on 12/11/2013).

Economists Staff Writers. 2012. "Pros and Cons: Mixed Bags," *The Economist*. http://www.economist.com/node/21542929, (last accessed on 12/13/2013).

Economists Staff Writers. 2012. "The rise of state capitalism," *The Economist*. http://www.economist.com/node/21543160, (last accessed on 12/13/2013).

Economists Staff Writers. 2013. "It's the politics, stupid," *The Economist*. http://www.economist.com/news/leaders/21574495-economy-faces-collapse-broader-based-government-needed-take-tough-decisions-its, (last accessed on 11/12/2013).

Economists Staff Writers. 2013. "Taking Europe's pulse," *The Economist*. http://www.economist.com/blogs/graphicdetail/2013/11/european-economy-guide, (last accessed on 12/13/2013).

Economists Staff Writers. 2013. "The perils of falling inflation," *The Economist*. http://www.economist.com/news/leaders/21589424-both-america-and-europe-central-bankers-should-be-pushing-prices-upwards-perils-falling, (last accessed on 11/12/2013).

Economists Staff Writers. 2013. "When giants slow down," *The Economist*. http://www.economist.com/news/briefing/21582257-most-dramatic-and-disruptive-period-emerging-market-growth-world-has-ever-seen, (last accessed on 12/13/2013).

Embassy of Colombia in Washington D.C. 2013. *About Colombia*. http://www.colombiaemb.org/overview, (last accessed on 10/30/2013).

Ernst & Young and Oxford Economics. 2011. *Trading Places: The Emergence of New Patterns of International Trade. Growing Beyond Series*. Ernst & Young and Oxford Economics.

Evans-Pritchard, Ambrose. 2013. "IMF sours on BRICs and doubts eurozone recovery claims," *The Telegraph*. http://www.telegraph.co.uk/finance/financial crisis/10365206/IMF-sours-on-BRICs-and-doubts-eurozone-recovery-claims.html, (last accessed on 11/08/2013).

Faulconbridge, G. 2008. "BRICs helped by Western finance crisis: Goldman," *Reuters*. http://www.reuters.com/article/2008/06/08/us-russia-forum-bric-idUSL071126420080608, (last accessed on 07/12/2012).

Forbes. 2000. "Global 2000." http://www.forbes.com/lists/2007/18/biz_07forbes 2000_The-Global-2000_Rank.html

Forbes. 2007. "Forbes' billionaire's." http://www.forbes.com/lists/2007/10/07 billionaires_The-Worlds-Billionaires_Rank.html

Foroohar, R. 2009. "BRICs Overtake G7 By 2027," *Newsweek*. http://www.newsweek.com/brics-overtake-g7-2027-76001, (last accessed on 04/12/2009).

Fox News Staff Writers. 2013. "IMF issues warning on South African economy," *Fox News*. http://www.foxnews.com/world/2013/10/01/imf-issues-warning-on-south-african-economy/, (last accessed on 10/24/2013).

Freeland, Chrystia. 2012. *Plutocrats: The Rise of the New Global Super-Rich And the Fall of Everyone Else*. New York, NY: Penguin Press.

Freeman, R. 2006. "The Great Doubling: The Challenge of the New Global Labor Market," *European Central Bank*. http://eml.berkeley.edu/~webfac/eichengreen/e183_sp07/great_doub.pdf, (last accessed on 11/02/2013).

Garcia-Herrero, Alicia. 2012. "BBVA EAGLES Emerging and Growth-Leading Economies," *BBVA Research*. http://www.bbvaresearch.com/KETD/fbin/mult/120215_BBVAEAGLES_Annual_Report_tcm348–288784.pdf?ts=1642012, (last accessed on 11/01/2013).

Garcia-Palafox, Galia. 2012. "Walmart Bribery Allegations: Watchdog Group Says Mexican Government Should Investigate Claims Of Vast Bribery Campaign," *Huffington Post*. http://www.huffingtonpost.com/2012/04/22/walmart-bribery-allegations-watchdog-urges-probe_n_1444488.html, (last accessed on 04/23/2012).

Geromel, Ricardo. 2013. "Forbes Top 10 Billionaire Cities - Moscow Beats New York Again," *Forbes*. http://www.forbes.com/sites/ricardogeromel/2013/03/14/forbes-top-10-billionaire-cities-moscow-beats-new-york-again/, (last accessed on 10/30/2013).

Ghanem, Hafez and Salman Shaikh. 2013. "On the Brink: Preventing Economic Collapse and Promoting Inclusive Growth in Egypt and Tunisia," *Brookings*. http://www.brookings.edu/research/papers/2013/11/economic-recovery-tunisia-egypt-shaikh-ghanem, (last accessed on 12/12/2013).

Ghosh A.R., M. Chamon, C. Crowe, J.I. Kim, and J.D. Ostry. 2009. "Coping with the Crisis: Policy Options for Emerging Market Countries," *International Monetary Fund*. http://www.imf.org/external/pubs/ft/spn/2009/spn0908.pdf, (last accessed on 12/12/2013).

GlobalEdge. 2013. "Market potential index (MPI) for emerging markets–2013," *Michigan State University*, International Business Center. Retrieved from http://globaledge.msu.edu/mpi

Golf Times. 2013. "US, eurozone deflation calls for 'expansionary policy'." http://www.gulf-times.com/business/191/details/374694/us,-eurozone-deflation-calls-for-'expansionary-policy', (last accessed on 07/23/2014).

Golf, E., R. Boccia, and J. Fleming. 2012. "Federal Spending per Household Is Skyrocketing, Federal Budget in Pictures," *The Heritage Foundation*. http://www.heritage.org/federalbudget/federal-spending-per-household, (last accessed on 01/23/2013).

Golf, E., R. Boccia, and J. Fleming. 2013. "2013 Index of Economic Freedom," *The Heritage Foundation*. http://www.heritage.org/index/ranking, (last accessed on 01/23/2013).

Grewal, Kevin. 2010. "CIVETS: The next gateway to growth," *Daily Markets*. http://www.dailymarkets.com/stock/2010/08/24/civets-the-next-gateway-to-growth/, (last accessed on 02/13/2011).

Gronholt-Pedersen, Jacob. 2012. "Cambodia Aims for Offshore Production Next Year." *The Wall Street Journal*. http://online.wsj.com/news/articles/SB10000872396390443507204578020023711640726, (last accessed on 02/11/2013).

Guerrera, Francesco. 2013. "Currency War Has Started." *The Wall Street Journal*. http://online.wsj.com/news/articles/SB100014241278873247610045782836841958922 50, (last accessed on 12/13/2013).

Halpin, Tony. 2009. "Brazil, Russia, India and China form bloc to challenge U.S. dominance," *The Times*. http://www.timesonline.co.uk/tol/news/world/us_and_americas/article6514737.ece, (last accessed on 23/03/2011).

Hamburger, T., B. Dennis, and J.L. Yang. 2012. "Wal-Mart took part in lobbying campaign to amend anti-bribery law," *The Washington Post*. http://www.washingtonpost.com/business/economy/wal-mart-took-part-in-lobbying-campaign-to-amend-anti-bribery-law/2012/04/24/gIQAyZcdfT_story_1.html, (last accessed on 11/19/2012).

Haub, Carl. 2012. "The BRIC Countries," *Population Reference Bureau*. http://www.prb.org/Publications/Articles/2012/brazil-russia-india-china.aspx, (last accessed on 12/05/2012).

Hauser, Christine. 2013. "Iraq: Maliki Demands That Protesters Stand Down," *The New York Times*. http://www.nytimes.com/2013/01/03/world/middleeast/iraq-maliki-demands-that-protesters-stand-down.html?_r=1&, (last accessed on 02/16/2013).

Hawksworth, J. 2011. "The world in 2005: How big will the major emerging market economies get and how can the OECD compete," *Price Waterhouse Coopers*. http://www.pwc.com/en_GX/gx/psrc/pdf/world_in_2050_carbon_emissions_psrc.pdf, (last accessed on 01/02/2011).

Hawksworth, John and Dan Chan. 2013. "World in 2050: The BRICS and Beyond: Prospects, Challenges, and Opportunities," *PWC Economics*. http://www.pwc.com/en_GX/gx/world-2050/assets/pwc-world-in-2050-report-january-2013.pdf, (last accessed on 03/12/2013).

Hayton, Bill. 2006. "Vietnam: ¿comunista o consumista?," *BBC Mundo*, Hanoi. http://news.bbc.co.uk/hi/spanish/business/newsid_5308000/5308298.stm, (last accessed on 07/22/2012).

Heng, Dyna. 2011. "Managing Cambodia's economic fragility," *CamproPost*. http://campropost.org/2011/07/15/managing-cambodia-s-economic-fragility.html, (last accessed on 10/10/2013).

Hood, Michael. 2013. "The Stubborn Inflation in Emerging Markets," *Institutional Investors*. http://www.institutionalinvestor.com/gmtl/3279243/The-Stubborn-Inflation-in-Emerging-Markets.html, (last accessed on 11/15/2013).

Hoti, Ikram. 2004. "Pakistan ends ties with IMF tomorrow," *PakistaniDefence.com*. http://forum.pakistanidefence.com/index.php?showtopic=36120, (last accessed on 10/12/2013).

HSBC Bank. 2013. "India Trade Forecast Report–HSBC Global Connections," *HSBC Global Connections Report*. India. https://globalconnections.hsbc.com/global/en/tools-data/trade-forecasts/in, (last accessed on 12/19/2013).

Human Rights Watch Staff Writers. 2012. "Iran: Arrest Sweeps Target Arab Minority," *Human Rights Watch*. http://www.refworld.org/docid/4f34de412.html, (last accessed on 11/03/2013).

Hutchinson, Martin. 2010. "The CIVETS: Windfall Wealth From the 'New' BRIC Economies," *European Business Review*. http://www.europeanbusinessreview.eu/page.asp?pid=829, (last accessed on 11/02/2013).

IMF Report. 2006. "Globalization and inflation," *World Economic Outlook*. Washington D.C. http://www.imf.org/external/pubs/ft/weo/2006/01/pdf/weo0406.pdf, (last accessed on 11/08/2013).

IMF Report. 2010a. Global Financial Stability Report. April.

IMF Report. 2013. "Economic Growth Moderates Across Middle East," *IMF Survey Magazine*. http://www.imf.org/external/pubs/ft/survey/so/2013/car052113a.htm, (last accessed on 01/03/2014).

IMF Report. 2013. "South Africa Searches for Faster Growth, More Jobs," *IMF Survey Magazine*. http://www.imf.org/external/pubs/ft/survey/so/2013/car080713a.htm, (last accessed on 11/05/2013).

IMF Report. 2013. "Transitions and tensions," *World Economic Outlook*. http://www.imf.org/external/pubs/ft/weo/2013/02/, (last accessed on 11/02/2013).

IMF Report. 2013. *World Economic Outlook*. http://www.imf.org/external/pubs/ft/weo/2013/01/weodata/index.aspx, (last accessed on 04/12/2013).

IMF Reports. 2013. Middle East and North Africa: Defining the Road Ahead, Regional Economic Outlook Update," *Middle East and Central Asia Department*.

http://www.imf.org/external/pubs/ft/reo/2013/mcd/eng/pdf/mcdreo 0513.pdf, (last accessed on 11/02/1013).

International News of Pakistan Staff Writers. 2012. "Asia Nations to Double Currency Swap Deal," *Pakistan.* http://www.thenews.com.pk/Todays-News-3–98519-Briefs, (last accessed on 11/05/2013).

Jahan, S. 2012. "Inflation Targeting: Holding the Line," *IMF.* Washington DC.

Jeong Chun Hai @Ibrahim, and Nor Fadzlina Nawi. 2007. *Principles of Public Administration: An Introduction.* Kuala Lumpur: Karisma Publications.

Johnson, A. G. 2000. *The Blackwell Dictionary of Sociology.* Oxford: Blackwell Publishing.

Khaithu. 2012. "Traditional Market in Vietnam: a Social and Economic Angle," 10/15/2012. http://khaithu.wordpress.com/2012/10/15/traditional-market-in-vn-a-social-and-economic-angle/, (last accessed on 11/01/2013).

Khanna, T., and K.G. Palepu. 2010. *Winning In Emerging Markets: A Roadmap for Strategy and Execution.* Boston, MA: Harvard Business School Publishing.

Koelbl, Susanne. 2011. "It Will Not Stop: Syrian Uprising Continues Despite Crackdown," *Der Spiegel.* http://www.spiegel.de/international/world/it-will-not-stop-syrian-uprising-continues-despite-crackdown-a-753517.html, (last accessed on 11/10/2013).

Kose, M.A., P. Loungani, and M.E. Terrones. 2012. "Tracking the Global Recovery," *IMF Finance and Development Magazine.* Vol. 49, No. 2.

Kowalczyk-Hoyer, Barbara and Susan Côté-Freeman. 2013. "Transparency in corporate reporting: Assessing emerging market multinationals," *Transparency International.* http://transparency.org/whatwedo/pub/transparency_in_corporate_reporting_assessing_emerging_market_multinational, (last accessed on 11/02/2013).

Lewis, P., A. Sen, and Z. Tabary. 2011. "New routes to the Middle East: Perspectives on inward investment and trade," *Economist Intelligence Unit.* https://www.business.hsbc.co.uk/1/PA_esf-ca-app-content/content/pdfs/en/new_routes_to_middle_east.pdf, (last accessed on 01/03/2014).

Lobe, Jim. 2013. "Scowcroft, Brzezinski Urge Iran Accord," *Lobe Log: Foreign Policy.* http://www.lobelog.com/scowcroft-brzezinski-urge-iran-accord/, (last accessed on 12/16/2013).

Manson, Katrina. 2011. "Pro-democracy protests reach Djibouti," *Financial Times.* http://www.ft.com/intl/cms/s/0/001f94f6–3d18–11e0-bbff-00144feabdc0.html?siteedition=intl, (last accessed on 10/25/2013).

Manyika, J., et al. 2012. "Manufacturing the future: The next era of global growth and innovation," *McKinsey Global Institute,* http://www.mckinsey.com/insights/manufacturing/the_future_of_manufacturing, (last accessed on 12/01/2013).

Markey, Patrick. 2010. "Colombia's Santos takes office with strong mandate," *Reuters.com.* http://www.reuters.com/article/2010/08/07/us-colombia-santos

-idUSTRE6760DD20100807, (last accessed on 10/30/2012).

Marquand, Robert. 2011. "Amid BRICS' rise and 'Arab Spring', a new global order forms," *Christian Science Monitor.* http://www.csmonitor.com/World/Global-Issues/2011/1018/Amid-BRICS-rise-and-Arab-Spring-a-new-global-order-forms, (last accessed 01/02/2013).

Matsui, Kathy. 2012. "A View from Japan," *Goldman Sachs.* http://www.youtube.com/watch?v=bfkqe4vLdFY, (last accessed on 11/10/2013).

Maxwell, John. 2012. "Beyond the BRICS: How to succeed in emerging markets (by really trying)," *PWC.* http://www.pwc.com/us/en/view/issue-15/succeed-emerging-markets.jhtml, (last accessed on 11/27/2013).

McCrummen, Stephanie. 2011. "13 killed in Iraq's 'Day of Rage' protests," *The Washington Post.* http://www.washingtonpost.com/wp-dyn/content/article/2011/02/24/AR2011022403117.html, (last accessed on 06/12/2011).

McKinnon, Ronald I. 1973. *Money and Capital in Economic Development.* Washington, DC: Brookings Institution Press.

Middle East Online Staff Writers. 2011. "Kuwaiti stateless protest for third day," *Middle East Online.* http://www.middle-east-online.com/english/?id=44476, (last accessed 10/25/2013).

Ministry of Economy and Finance of Cambodia. 2013. "Council for the development of Cambodia (CDC)," *Economic Trends.* http://www.cambodiainvestment.gov.kh/investment-enviroment/economic-trend.html, (last accessed on 11/04/2013).

Mitchell, Jared. 2013. "Why Emerging Markets are tough to enter," *HSBC Global Connections.* https://globalconnections.hsbc.com/canada/en/articles/why-emerging-markets-are-tough-enter, (last accessed on 12/16/2013).

Moghadam, Reza. 2010. "How Did Emerging Markets Cope in the Crisis?, The Strategy, Policy, and Review Department, in consultation with other IMF departments," *IMF.* http://www.imf.org/external/np/pp/eng/2010/061510.pdf, (last accessed on 11/15/2013).

Montibeler, E.E., and E.S. Gallego. 2012. "Relaciones Bilaterales Entre Brasily Liga Árabe: Un Análisis a Partir de la Teoría de la Internacionalización de la Producción y de la Diversificación Comercial." *Observatorio de la Economía Latinoamericana,* 163.

Mookerji, Nivedita. 2013. "Walmart continues to bide its time over Bharti investment," *Business Standard.* http://www.business-standard.com/article/companies/walmart-continues-to-bide-its-time-over-bharti-investment-113081600670_1.html, (last accessed on 12/15/2013).

Moore, M. 2005. "Signposts to More Effective States: Responding to Governance Challenges in Developing Countries," *Institute of Developing Studies, The Centre for the Future State, UK,* http://www2.ids.ac.uk/gdr/cfs/pdfs/SignpoststoMoreEffectiveStates.pdf, (last accessed on 12/10/2013).

Mortished, Carl. 2008. "Russia shows its political clout by hosting BRIC summit." *The Times*. http://www.thetimes.co.uk/tto/business/markets/russia/article2143017.ece, (last accessed on 05/12/2012).

Mutum, D.P., S.K. Roy, and E. Kipnis (Eds). 2014. *Marketing Cases From Emerging Markets*. New York, NY: Springer.

Nath, Ravindra. 2011. "Qaboos fires 10 ministers," *Khaleej Times*, Muscat, UAE. http://www.khaleejtimes.com/displayarticle.asp?xfile=data/middleeast/2011/March/middleeast_March140.xml&section=middleeast&col=, (last accessed on 10/12/2013).

New York City Bar Association. 2011. "The FCPA and its Impact on International Business Transactions—Should Anything be Done to Minimize the Consequences of the U.S.'s Unique Position on Combating Offshore Corruption?," *New York City Bar Association*. http://www2.nycbar.org/pdf/report/uploads/FCPAImpactonInternationalBusinessTransactions.pdf, (last accessed on 12/18/2013).

Nilekani, Nandan. 2008. *Imagining India: The Idea of a Renewed Nation*. New York City, NY: Penguin Group.

O'Neill, J. 2011. *The Growth Map: Economic Opportunity in the BRICs and Beyond*. Penguin Group.

O'Neill, Jim. 2001. "Building Better Global Economic BRICs," *Global Economics Paper No. 66*, Goldman Sachs. http://www.goldmansachs.com/our-thinking/archive/archive-pdfs/build-better-brics.pdf, (last accessed on 12/17/2011).

O'Neill, Jim. 2005. "How solid are the BRICS," *Goldman Sachs' Global Economics Paper No. 134*. http://www.goldmansachs.com/our-thinking/archive/archive-pdfs/how-solid.pdf, (last accessed on 11/14/2012).

O'Sullivan, A., M.E. Rey, and M.J. Galvez. 2011. "Opportunities and Challenges in the MENA Region." *The Arab world competitiveness report, 2011–2012, World Economic Forum*. http://www.weforum.org/reports/arab-world-competitiveness-report-2011–2012, (last accessed on 01/02/2014).

OECD. 2007. Overview by the DAC Chair. In *Development Co-operation Report*. Vol. 8(1), chapter 1 (Paris, France: OECD, 2007).

Organization for Economic Co-operation and Development. 2013. "Economic outlook: analysis and forecast: Turkey Economic forecast summary, May 2014," *OECD*, http://www.oecd.org/eco/outlook/turkey-economic-forecast-summary.htm, (last accessed on 11/04/2013).

Organization for Economic Co-operation and Development. 2013. "Economic surveys and country surveillance: Economic Survey of Japan 2013," *OECD*. http://www.oecd.org/eco/surveys/economic-survey-japan.htm, (last accessed on 11/05/2013).

Organization for Economic Co-operation and Development. 2013. "Economic surveys and country surveillance: Economic Survey of South Africa 2013,"

OECD, http://www.oecd.org/eco/surveys/economic-survey-south-africa.htm, (last accessed on 11/05/2103).

Orgaz, L., L. Molina and C. Carrasco. 2011. "In El Creciente Peso de las Economias Emergentes en la Economia y Gobernanza Mundiales, Los Paises BRIC," *Documentos Ocasionales numero 1101*, Banco de Espana, Eurosistema. http://www.bde.es/f/webbde/SES/Secciones/Publicaciones/Publicaciones Seriadas/DocumentosOcasionales/11/Fich/do1101.pdf, (last accessed on 12/12/12).

Oxford Business Group's Staff Writers. 2013. "Brunei Darussalam looks to its labs for growth," *Brunei Darussalam,* http://www.oxfordbusinessgroup.com/ economic_updates/brunei-darussalam-looks-its-labs-growth, (last accessed on 11/02/2013).

Pacek, N. and D. Thorniley. 2007. *Emerging Markets: Lessons for Business and the Outlook for Different Markets (2nd edition).* London: The Economist and Profile Books.

Pain, N., I. Koske, and M. Sollie. 2006. "Globalization and inflation in the OECD Economies," *Economics Department Working Paper No. 524,* OECD, Paris. http://www.oecd.org/eco/42503918.pdf, (last retrieved on 11/12/2013).

Papademos, Lucas. 2006. "Globalization, inflation, imbalances and monetary policy," *Bank for International Settlement,* St. Louis, U.S., http://www.bis.org/ review/r060607d.pdf, (last accessed on 11/09/2013).

Peterson, S. 2011. "Egypt's Revolution Redefines What's Possible in the Arab World," *The Christian Science Monitor,* http://www.csmonitor.com/layout/ set/r14/World/Middle-East/2011/0211/Egypt-s-revolution-redefines-what-s-possible-in-the-Arab-world, (last accessed on 11/10/2013).

Pettis, Michael. 2013. *The Great Rebalancing: Trade, Conflict, and the Perilous Road Ahead for the World Economy.* Princeton University Press.

Pigato, Miria. 2009. *Strengthening China's and India's Trade and Investment Ties to the Middle East and North Africa.* Washington, DC: The World Bank.

Portes, R. 2010. *Currency Wars and the Emerging-Market Countries. Vox*EU, http:// www.voxeu.org/article/currency-wars-and-emerging-markets, (last accessed on 6/25/2014)

Posadas, Alejandro. 2000. "Combating Corruption Under International Law," *Duke University Journal of Comparative and International Law,* pp. 345–414, http:// scholarship.law.duke.edu/djcil/vol10/iss2/4, (last accessed on 12/02/2013).

Qiang, Hou. 2013. "ASEAN businesses see integration as opportunity, not threat: survey," *The English News,* Xinhua, China, http://news.xinhuanet.com/english/ business/2013–12/11/c_132960344.htm, (last accessed on 12/11/2013).

Radu, Paul C. 2008. "The Investigative Journalist Handbook," *International Center for Journalist,* https://reportingproject.net/occrp/index.php/en/cc-resource-center/handbook/191-the-investigative-journalist-handbook, (last accessed on 09/08/2012).

Rai, V. and W. Simon. 2008. *Think India*. New York, NY: Penguin Group.

Rashid, Ahmed, (2012) *Pakistan on the Brink: The Future of America, Pakistan, and Afghanistan*. New York, NY: Viking/Penguin Group.

Reinhart, C.M. and M.B. Sbrancia. 2011. "The Liquidation of Government Debt," *NBER Working Paper 16893*. http://www.nber.org/papers/w16893, (last retrieved 03/02/2012).

Reinhart, C.M. and J.F. Kirkegaard. 2012. "Financial Repression: Then and Now," *Vox*, http://www.voxeu.org/article/financial-repression-then-and-now, (last accessed on 04/23/2012).

Rich, Ben R. and Leo Janos. 1994. *Skunk Works: A Personal Memoir of My Years at Lockheed*. New York: Little Brown & Co., 1994, p. 10.

Richter, Frederick. 2011. "Protester killed in Bahrain 'Day of Rage'," *Reuters,* http://uk.reuters.com/article/2011/02/14/uk-bahrain-protests-idUKTRE71D1G5 20110214, (last accessed on 11/02/2013).

Rickards, J. 2011. *Currency Wars: The Making of the Next Global Crisis*, Penguin/Portfolio Group.

Rodrik, D. 2009. *Growth after the Crisis*. Cambridge, MA.: Harvard Kennedy School.

Roudi, Farzaneh. 2001. "Population Trends and Challenges in the MENA," *PRB*. http://www.prb.org/Publications/Reports/2001/PopulationTrendsand Challen-gesintheMiddleEastandNorthAfrica.aspx, (last accessed on 12/20/2013).

RT Staff Writers. 2013. "BRICS agree to capitalize development bank at $100bn," *RT,* http://rt.com/business/russia-brics-bank-g20-468/, (last accessed on 11/06/2013).

Sallum, M.N. 2013. "Potencial a explorar é enorme." *Agência de Notícias Brasil-Árabe.* http://www.anba.com.br/, (last accessed on 01/03/2014).

Schmidt, V. 2003. "French Capitalism Transformed; yet still a Third Variety of Capitalism." *Economy and Society*, 32(4). http://www.vedegylet.hu/fejkrit/szvggyujt/schmidt_frenchCapitalism.pdf

Schwab, Klaus. 2013. "The Global Competitiveness Report 2012–2013," *World Economic Forum*, http://www3.weforum.org/docs/WEF_GlobalCompetitive nessReport_2012–13.pdf, (last accessed on 08/12/2013).

Schwartz, Nelson. 2013. "Growth Gain Blurs Signs of Weakness in Economy," *New York Times*, http://www.nytimes.com/2013/11/08/business/economy/us-economy-grows-at-2–8-rate-in-third-quarter.html?_r=0, (last accessed on 11/10/2013).

Senkovich, V. 2013. "The Arab World's Potential Importance to Russia's Economy." *Russian International Affairs Council.* http://russiancouncil.ru/en/inner/?id_4=1548#top, (last accessed on 01/03/2014).

Seyid, Seyid Ould. 2011. "Mauritania police crush protest—doctors announce strike," *Radio Netherlands Worldwide*, Africa Desk, Mauritania. http://www.rnw.nl/africa/article/mauritania-police-crush-protest-doctors-announce-strike, (last retrieved on 12/12/2012).

Shahminan, Fitri. 2013. "Brunei economy to grow 2.4pc in next four years," *Dawn. com*, http://www.dawn.com/news/1048280/brunei-economy-to-grow-24pc-in-next-four-years, (last accessed on 10/10/2013).

Smith & Nephew Corporate. 2012. "Smith & Nephew reaches settlement with US Government," *Smith & Nephew*, http://www.smith-nephew.com/news-and-media/news/smith-and-nephew-reaches-settlement-with-us-gover/, (last accessed on 12/12/2013).

Snyder, Michael. 2012. "45 Signs That China Is Colonizing America," *End of The American Dream*, http://endoftheamericandream.com/archives/45-signs-that-china-is-colonizing-america, (last accessed on 09/08/2013).

Soubbotina, Tatyana P. and Katherine A. Sheram. 2004. *Beyond Economic Growth: An Introduction to Sustainable Development*, World Bank, 2nd edition.

Spencer, R., 2011. "Libya: civil war breaks out as Gaddafi mounts rearguard fight," *The Telegraph*, http://www.telegraph.co.uk/news/worldnews/africaandindianocean/libya/8344034/Libya-civil-war-breaks-out-as-Gaddafi-mounts-rearguard-fight.html, (last accessed on 11/12/2013).

Stout, David. 2009. "Ex-Rep. Jefferson Convicted in Bribery Scheme," *The New York Times*, p. A14, http://www.nytimes.com/2009/08/06/us/06jefferson.html, (last accessed on 06/14/2013).

Stern, Melanie. 2012. "International Trade: CIVETS Economies," *Financial Director Newspaper*, London, UK. http://www.financialdirector.co.uk/financial-director/feature/2169190/international-trade-civets-economies, (last accessed on 11/03/2013).

Svensson, L.E.O. 2008. "Inflation Targeting," in S.N. Durlauf & L.E. Blume (Eds.), *The New Palgrave Dictionary of Economics, 2nd edition*. Palgrave Macmillan.

Taborda, Joana. 2013. "Death of the Dollar 2014: Euro Area GDP Growth Rate," *Trading Economics*, http://www.tradingeconomics.com/euro-area/gdp-growth, (last accessed on 12/15/2013).

Telegraph Staff Writers. 2013. "Next chief Lord Wolfson launches £250,000 prize to solve housing crisis." *The Telegraph*, http://www.telegraph.co.uk/finance/newsbysector/constructionandproperty/10448303/Next-chief-Lord-Wolfson-launches-250000-prize-to-solve-housing-crisis.html, (last accessed on 12/11/2013).

The FCPA Blog. 2012, "Biomet Pays $22.8 Million To Settle Bribe Charges," *The FCPA Blog*, http://www.fcpablog.com/blog/2012/3/26/biomet-pays-228-million-to-settle-bribe-charges.html, (last accessed on 09/09/2012).

Transparency International Secretariat. 2013. "Media advisory: Major exporters still lag in enforcing rules against foreign bribery," *Transparency International*, http://www.transparency.org/news/pressrelease/bribe_paying_still_very_high_worldwide_but_people_ready_to_fight_back, (last accessed on 12/14/2013).

U.S. Department of Justice. 2012. "Marubeni Corporation Resolves Foreign Corrupt Practices Act Investigation and Agrees to Pay a $54.6 Million Criminal Penalty," *U.S. Department of Justice,* http://www.justice.gov/opa/pr/2012/January/12-crm-060.html, (last accessed on 07/02/2013).

Vaidya, Sunil. 2011. "One dead, dozens injured as Oman protest turns ugly," *Gulf News,* Oman, http://gulfnews.com/news/gulf/oman/one-dead-dozen-injured-as-oman-protest-turns-ugly-1.768789, (last accessed on 11/01/2013).

Vale Columbia Center on Sustainable International Investment. 2009. "First ranking survey of Mexican multinationals finds grey diversity of industries," *Columbia Law School,* http://www.vcc.columbia.edu/files/vale/documents/EMGP-Mexico-Report-Final-09Dec09.pdf, (last accessed on 11/30/2013).

Wagstyl, S. 2013. "Eurasia: emerging markets are world's 'top risk' for 2013," *Financial Times,* http://blogs.ft.com/beyond-brics/2013/01/07/eurasia-emerging-markets-are-worlds-top-risk-for-2013/#axzz2nkpeGUB7, (last accessed on 12/17/2013).

Weggel, Oskar. 2006. "Cambodia in 2005: Year of Reassurance." *Asian Survey* 46(1): 158.

Welch, D. and T. Weidlich. 2012. "Wal-Mart Bribery Probe May Exposes Retailer to U.S. Fines," *Bloomberg,* http://www.bloomberg.com/news/2012–04-23/wal-mart-bribery-probe-may-exposes-retailer-to-u-s-fines.html, (last accessed on 04/23/2012).

Werr, Patrick. 2013. "Egypt's economy to miss government growth forecasts: Reuters poll," *Reuters* Cairo, Egypt, http://www.reuters.com/article/2013/10/01/us-economy-egypt-poll-idUSBRE99012O20131001, (last accessed on 10/30/2013).

Wheatley, Alan. 2013. "Emerging markets thrive as eurozone suffers," *The International News,* http://www.thenews.com.pk/Todays-News-3–167386-Emerging-markets-thrive-as-eurozone-suffers, (last accessed on 11/10/2013).

Williams, R. 1983. *Capitalism (Revised Edition).* Oxford: Oxford University Press.

Wilson, D. and R. Purushothaman. 2003. "Dreaming with BRICs: The Path to 2050," *Global Economics Paper No. 99,* Goldman Sachs,, http://www.goldmansachs.com/our-thinking/archive/archive-pdfs/brics-dream.pdf, (last accessed on 04/05/11).

World Bank Staff Writers. 2013. "Tourism in the Arab World can mean more than Sun, Sand and Beaches," *The World Bank,* http://www.worldbank.org/en/news/feature/2013/02/11/tourism-in-the-arab-world-can-mean-more-than-sun-sand-and-beaches, (last accessed on 01/03/2014).

World Bank Staff Writers. 2012. "Doing Business 2014: Ease of Doing Business in Pakistan," *The World Bank.* http://www.doingbusiness.org/data/exploreeconomies/pakistan, (last accessed on 11/10/2012).

World Bank Staff Writers. 2012. "World Development Indicators Database. Gross Domestic Product 2011," *The World Bank*, http://data.worldbank.org/data-catalog/world-development-indicators, (last accessed on 09/22/2012).

World Bank Staff Writers. 2013. "An Update on Vietnam's Recent Economic Development July 2013: Key Findings," *The World Bank*, http://www.worldbank.org/en/news/feature/2013/07/12/taking-stock-july-2013-an-update-on-vietnams-recent-economic-development-key-findings, (last accessed on 11/05/2013).

World Bank Staff Writers. 2013. "Doing Business: Ease of Doing Business in Colombia," *The World Bank*, http://www.doingbusiness.org/data/exploreeconomies/colombia/, (last accessed on 06/12/2013).

World Bank. 2013. "Doing Business: Measuring Business Regulations," *The World Bank*, http://www.doingbusiness.org/rankings, (last accessed on 09/22/2012).

World Bank. 2008. *Middle East and North Africa Region 2007 Economic Developments and Prospects: Job Creation in an Era of High Growth.* Washington, DC: World Bank. http://documents.worldbank.org/curated/en/2008/06/9520526/middle-east-north-africa-region-2007-economic-developments-prospects-job-creation-era-high-growth, (last accessed on 6/29/2014).

Young, V. 2006. "Macquarie launches Australia's first BRIC funds," *InvestorDaily*, http://www.investordaily.com.au/25542-macquarie-launches-australias-first-bric-funds, (last accessed on 05/23/2007).

Zoffer, Joshua. 2012. "Future of Dollar Hegemony," *The Harvard International Review*, http://hir.harvard.edu/crafting-the-city/future-of-dollar-hegemony, (last accessed on 10/12/2012).

Index

OTHER TITLES FROM THE ECONOMICS COLLECTION

Philip Romero, The University of Oregon and Jeffrey Edwards,
North Carolina A&T State University, Editors

- *Game Theory: Anticipating Reactions for Winning Actions* by Mark L. Burkey
- *A Primer on Macroeconomics* by Thomas Beveridge
- *Economic Decision Making Using Cost Data: A Guide for Managers*
  by Daniel Marburger
- *The Fundamentals of Money and Financial Systems* by Shahdad Naghshpour
- *International Economics: Understanding the Forces of Globalization for Managers*
  by Paul Torelli
- *The Economics of Crime* by Zagros Madjd-Sadjadi
- *Money and Banking: An Intermediate Market-Based Approach* by William D. Gerdes
- *Basel III Liquidity Regulation and Its Implications* by Mark A. Petersen
  and Janine Mukuddem-Petersen
- *Saving American Manufacturing: The Fight for Jobs, Opportunity, and National Security*
  by William R. Killingsworth
- *What Hedge Funds Really Do: An Introduction to Portfolio Management* by Philip J.
  Romero and Tucker Balch
- *Advanced Economies and Emerging Markets: Prospects for Globalization*
  by Marcus Goncalves, José Alves, Carlos Frota, Harry Xia, and Rajabahadur V. Arcot
- *Comparing Emerging and Advanced Markets: Current Trends and Challenges*
  by Marcus Goncalves and Harry Xia
- *Learning Basic Macroeconomics: A Policy Perspective from Different Schools of Thought*
  by Hal W. Snarr
- *Emerging and Frontier Markets: The New Frontline for Global Trade* by Marcus Goncalves
  and José Alves

Announcing the Business Expert Press Digital Library

*Concise E-books Business Students Need
for Classroom and Research*

This book can also be purchased in an e-book collection by your library as
- a one-time purchase,
- that is owned forever,
- allows for simultaneous readers,
- has no restrictions on printing, and
- can be downloaded as PDFs from within the library community.

Our digital library collections are a great solution to beat the rising cost of textbooks. E-books can be loaded into their course management systems or onto students' e-book readers.
The **Business Expert Press** digital libraries are very affordable, with no obligation to buy in future years. For more information, please visit **www.businessexpertpress.com/librarians**. To set up a trial in the United States, please email **sales@businessexpertpress.com**.

CPSIA information can be obtained at www.ICGtesting.com
Printed in the USA
BVOW03s0323041114

372977BV00004BA/5/P